Cambridge IELTS 4

Examination papers from University of Cambridge ESOL Examinations: English for Speakers of Other Languages

CAMBRIDGE
UNIVERSITY PRESS

CAMBRIDGE UNIVERSITY PRESS
Cambridge, New York, Melbourne, Madrid, Cape Town, Singapore, São Paulo, Delhi

Cambridge University Press
The Edinburgh Building, Cambridge CB2 8RU, UK

www.cambridge.org
Information on this title: www.cambridge.org/9780521544627

First published 2005
5th printing 2009

Printed in the United Kingdom at the University Press, Cambridge

A catalogue record for this publication is available from the British Library

ISBN 978-0-521-54462-7 Student's Book with answers
ISBN 978-0-521-54464-1 cassette set
ISBN 978-0-521-54465-8 CD set (audio)
ISBN 978-0-521-54463-4 Self-study Pack

Contents

Introduction

The International English Language Testing System (IELTS) is widely recognised as a reliable means of assessing whether candidates are ready to study or train in the medium of English. These Practice Tests are designed to give future IELTS candidates an idea of whether their English is at the required level.

IELTS is owned by three partners, the University of Cambridge ESOL Examinations, the British Council and IDP Education Australia (through its subsidiary company, IELTS Australia Pty Limited).

Further information on IELTS can be found in the IELTS Handbook, available free of charge from IELTS centres.

WHAT IS THE TEST FORMAT?

IELTS consists of six modules. All candidates take the same Listening and Speaking modules. There is a choice of Reading and Writing modules according to whether a candidate is taking the Academic or General Training version of the test.

Academic	General Training
For candidates taking the test for entry to undergraduate or postgraduate studies or for professional reasons.	For candidates taking the test for entry to vocational or training programmes not at degree level, for admission to secondary schools and for immigration purposes.

The test modules are taken in the following order:

Listening		
4 sections, 40 items		
30 minutes		
Academic Reading		**General Training Reading**
3 sections, 40 items	OR	3 sections, 40 items
60 minutes		60 minutes
Academic Writing		**General Training Writing**
2 tasks	OR	2 tasks
60 minutes		60 minutes
Speaking		
11 to 14 minutes		
Total test time		
2 hours 44 minutes		

Listening

This module consists of four sections, each with 10 questions. The first two sections are concerned with social needs. There is a conversation between two speakers and then a monologue. The final two sections are concerned with situations related to educational or training contexts. There is a conversation between up to four people and then a monologue.

A variety of question types is used, including: multiple choice, short-answer questions, sentence completion, notes/form/table/summary/flow-chart/timetable completion, labelling a diagram/plan/map, classification, matching.

Candidates hear the recording once only and answer the questions as they listen. Ten minutes are allowed at the end for candidates to transfer their answers to the answer sheet.

Academic Reading

This module consists of three sections with 40 questions. There are three reading passages, which are taken from magazines, journals, books and newspapers. The passages are on topics of general interest. At least one text contains detailed logical argument.

A variety of question types is used, including: multiple choice, short-answer questions, sentence completion, notes/summary/flow-chart/table completion, labelling a diagram, classification, matching, choosing suitable paragraph headings from a list, identification of writer's views/claims – yes, no, not given – or identification of information in the text – true, false, not given.

General Training Reading

This module consists of three sections with 40 questions. The texts are taken from notices, advertisements, leaflets, newspapers, instruction manuals, books and magazines. The first section contains texts relevant to basic linguistic survival in English, with tasks mainly concerned with providing factual information. The second section focuses on the training context and involves texts of more complex language. The third section involves reading more extended texts, with a more complex structure, but with the emphasis on descriptive and instructive rather than argumentative texts.

Various question types are used, including: multiple choice, short-answer questions, sentence completion, notes/summary/flow-chart/table completion, labelling a diagram, classification, matching, choosing suitable paragraph headings from a list, identification of writer's views/claims – yes, no, not given – or identification of information in the text – true, false, not given.

Academic Writing

This module consists of two tasks. It is suggested that candidates spend about 20 minutes on Task 1, which requires them to write at least 150 words, and 40 minutes on Task 2, which requires them to write at least 250 words. The assessment of Task 2 carries more weight in marking than Task 1.

Task 1 requires candidates to look at a diagram or some data (graph, table or chart) and to present the information in their own words. They may be assessed on their ability to organise, present and possibly compare data, describe the stages of a process, describe an object or event, or explain how something works.

In Task 2 candidates are presented with a point of view, argument or problem. They are assessed on their ability to present a solution to the problem, present and justify an opinion, compare and contrast evidence and opinions, and evaluate and challenge ideas, evidence or arguments.

Candidates are also assessed on their ability to write in an appropriate style.

General Training Writing

This module consists of two tasks. It is suggested that candidates spend about 20 minutes on Task 1, which requires them to write at least 150 words, and 40 minutes on Task 2, which requires them to write at least 250 words. The assessment of Task 2 carries more weight in marking than Task 1.

In Task 1 candidates are asked to respond to a given problem with a letter requesting information or explaining a situation. They are assessed on their ability to engage in personal correspondence, elicit and provide general factual information, express needs, wants, likes and dislikes, and express opinions, complaints, etc.

In Task 2 candidates are presented with a point of view, argument or problem. They are assessed on their ability to provide general factual information, outline a problem and present a solution, present and justify an opinion, and evaluate and challenge ideas, evidence or arguments.

Candidates are also assessed on their ability to write in an appropriate style.

Speaking

This module consists of an oral interview between the candidate and an examiner. It takes between 11 and 14 minutes.

There are three parts:

Part 1
The candidate and the examiner introduce themselves. Candidates then answer general questions about themselves, their home/family, their job/studies, their interests and a wide range of similar familiar topic areas. This part lasts between four and five minutes.

Part 2
The candidate is given a task card with prompts and is asked to talk on a particular topic. The candidate has one minute to prepare and they can make some notes if they wish, before speaking for between one and two minutes. The examiner then asks one or two rounding-off questions.

Part 3
The examiner and the candidate engage in a discussion of more abstract issues which are thematically linked to the topic prompt in Part 2. The discussion lasts between four and five minutes.

The Speaking module assesses whether candidates can communicate effectively in English. The assessment takes into account Fluency and Coherence, Lexical Resource, Grammatical Range and Accuracy, and Pronunciation.

HOW IS IELTS SCORED?

IELTS results are reported on a nine-band scale. In addition to the score for overall language ability, IELTS provides a score in the form of a profile for each of the four skills (Listening, Reading, Writing and Speaking). These scores are also reported on a nine-band scale. All scores are recorded on the Test Report Form along with details of the candidate's nationality, first language and date of birth. Each Overall Band Score corresponds to a descriptive statement which gives a summary of the English language ability of a candidate classified at that level. The nine bands and their descriptive statements are as follows:

9 Expert User – *Has fully operational command of the language: appropriate, accurate and fluent with complete understanding.*

8 Very Good User – *Has fully operational command of the language with only occasional unsystematic inaccuracies and inappropriacies. Misunderstandings may occur in unfamiliar situations. Handles complex detailed argumentation well.*

7 Good User – *Has operational command of the language, though with occasional inaccuracies, inappropriacies and misunderstandings in some situations. Generally handles complex language well and understands detailed reasoning.*

6 Competent User – *Has generally effective command of the language despite some inaccuracies, inappropriacies and misunderstandings. Can use and understand fairly complex language, particularly in familiar situations.*

5 Modest User – *Has partial command of the language, coping with overall meaning in most situations, though is likely to make many mistakes. Should be able to handle basic communication in own field.*

4 Limited User – *Basic competence is limited to familiar situations. Has frequent problems in understanding and expression. Is not able to use complex language.*

3 Extremely Limited User – *Conveys and understands only general meaning in very familiar situations. Frequent breakdowns in communication occur.*

2 Intermittent User – *No real communication is possible except for the most basic information using isolated words or short formulae in familiar situations and to meet immediate needs. Has great difficulty understanding spoken and written English.*

1 Non User – *Essentially has no ability to use the language beyond possibly a few isolated words.*

0 Did not attempt the test. – *No assessable information provided.*

Most universities and colleges in the United Kingdom, Australia, New Zealand and Canada accept an IELTS Overall Band Score of 6.0 or 6.5 for entry to academic programmes. IELTS scores are recognised by over 500 universities and colleges in the USA.

MARKING THE PRACTICE TESTS

Listening and Reading

The Answer key is on pages 152–161.

Each question in the Listening and Reading modules is worth one mark.

Questions which require letter/Roman numeral answers
- For questions where the answers are letters or Roman numerals, you should write *only* the number of answers required. If you have written more letters or numerals than are required, the answer must be marked wrong.

Questions which require answers in the form of words or numbers
- Answers may be written in upper or lower case.
- Words in brackets are *optional* – they are correct, but not necessary.
- Alternative answers are separated by a single slash (/).
- If you are asked to write an answer using a certain number of words and/or (a) number(s), you will be penalised if you exceed this. For example, if a question specifies an answer using NO MORE THAN THREE WORDS and the correct answer is 'black leather coat', the answer 'coat of black leather' is *incorrect*.
- In questions where you are expected to complete a gap, you should only transfer the necessary missing word(s) onto the answer sheet. For example, to complete 'in the . . .', where the correct answer is 'morning', the answer 'in the morning' would be *incorrect*.
- All answers require correct spelling (including words in brackets).
- Both US and UK spelling are acceptable and are included in the Answer key.
- All standard alternatives for numbers, dates and currencies are acceptable.
- All standard abbreviations are acceptable.
- You will find additional notes about individual questions in the Answer key.

Writing

It is not possible for you to give yourself a mark for the Writing tasks. For *Task 1* in *Tests 1* and *3*, and *Task 2* in *Tests 2* and *4* and *General Training Test B* we have provided *model answers* (written by an examiner) at the back of the book. It is important to note that these show just one way of completing the task, out of many possible approaches. For *Task 2* in *Tests 1* and *3*, and *Task 1* in *Tests 2* and *4* and *General Training Test A*, we have provided *sample answers* (written by candidates), showing their score and the examiner's comments. These model answers and sample answers will give you an insight into what is required for the Writing module.

HOW SHOULD YOU INTERPRET YOUR SCORES?

In the Answer key at the end of each set of Listening and Reading answers you will find a chart which will help you assess whether, on the basis of your Practice Test results, you are ready to take the IELTS exam.

In interpreting your score, there are a number of points you should bear in mind. Your performance in the real IELTS exam will be reported in two ways: there will be a Band Score from 1 to 9 for each of the modules and an Overall Band Score from 1 to 9, which is the average of your scores in the four modules. However, institutions considering your application are advised to look at both the Overall Band Score and the Band scores for each module in order to determine whether you have the language skills needed for a particular course of study. For example, if your course has a lot of reading and writing, but no lectures, listening skills might be less important and a score of 5 in Listening might be acceptable if the Overall Band Score was 7. However, for a course which has lots of lectures and spoken instructions, a score of 5 in Listening might be unacceptable even though the Overall Band Score was 7.

Once you have marked your tests you should have some idea of whether your listening and reading skills are good enough for you to try the IELTS exam. If you did well enough in one module but not in others, you will have to decide for yourself whether you are ready to take the exam.

The Practice Tests have been checked to ensure that they are of approximately the same level of difficulty as the real IELTS exam. However, we cannot guarantee that your score in the Practice Tests will be reflected in the real IELTS exam. The Practice Tests can only give you an idea of your possible future performance and it is ultimately up to you to make decisions based on your score.

Different institutions accept different IELTS scores for different types of courses. We have based our recommendations on the average scores which the majority of institutions accept. The institution to which you are applying may, of course, require a higher or lower score than most other institutions.

Sample answers and model answers are provided for the Writing tasks. The sample answers were written by IELTS candidates; each answer has been given a band score and the candidate's performance is described. Please note that there are many different ways by which a candidate may achieve a particular band score. The model answers were written by an examiner as examples of very good answers, but it is important to understand that they are just one example out of many possible approaches.

Further information

For more information about IELTS or any other University of Cambridge ESOL examination write to:

University of Cambridge ESOL Examinations
1 Hills Road
Cambridge
CB1 2EU
United Kingdom

Telephone: +44 1223 553311
Fax: +44 1223 460278
e-mail: ESOLhelpdesk@ucles.org.uk
http://www.cambridgeesol.org
http://www.ielts.org

Test 1

SECTION 1   *Questions 1–10*

Questions 1–4

Complete the notes below.

*Write **NO MORE THAN THREE WORDS AND/OR A NUMBER** for each answer.*

NOTES ON SOCIAL PROGRAMME

Example	*Answer*
Number of trips per month:	**5**
	....

Visit places which have:

- historical interest

- good **1** ....

- **2** ....

Cost:	between £5.00 and £15.00 per person
Note:	special trips organised for groups of **3** .... people
Time:	departure – 8.30 a.m. return – 6.00 p.m.
To reserve a seat:	sign name on the **4** .... 3 days in advance

Questions 5–10

Complete the table below.

Write **NO MORE THAN THREE WORDS AND/OR A NUMBER** *for each answer.*

WEEKEND TRIPS			
Place	**Date**	**Number of seats**	**Optional extra**
St Ives	**5**	16	Hepworth Museum
London	16th February	45	**6** ....
7	3rd March	18	S.S. *Great Britain*
Salisbury	18th March	50	Stonehenge
Bath	23rd March	16	**8** ....
For further information: Read the **9** .... or see Social Assistant: Jane **10**			

SECTION 2   *Questions 11–20*

Questions 11–13

Complete the sentences below.

*Write **NO MORE THAN THREE WORDS AND/OR A NUMBER** for each answer.*

RIVERSIDE INDUSTRIAL VILLAGE

11   Riverside Village was a good place to start an industry because it had water, raw materials and fuels such as .... and ....

12   The metal industry was established at Riverside Village by .... who lived in the area.

13   There were over .... water-powered mills in the area in the eighteenth century.

Questions 14–20

Label the plan below.

*Write **NO MORE THAN TWO WORDS** for each answer.*

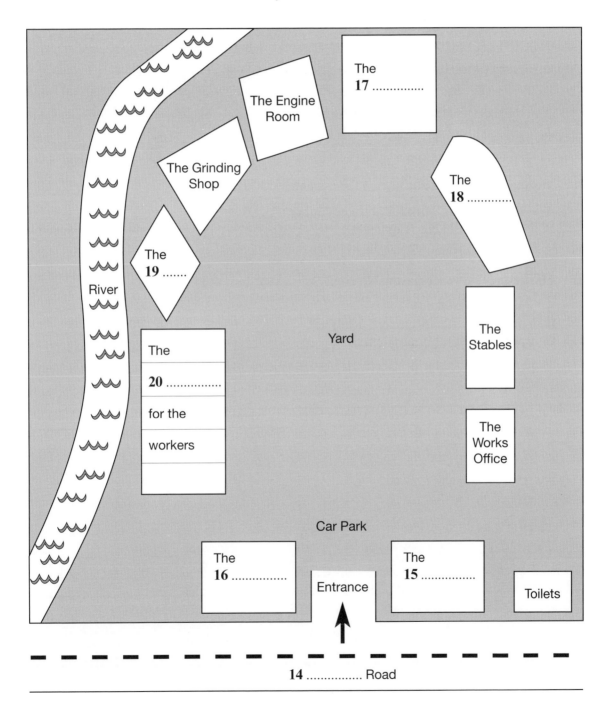

SECTION 3   *Questions 21–30*

Questions 21 and 22

Choose the correct letter, A, B or C.

Example

Melanie could not borrow any books from the library because

    A   the librarian was out.
    B   she didn't have time to look.
    Ⓒ   the books had already been borrowed.

---

21   Melanie says she has not started the assignment because

    A   she was doing work for another course.
    B   it was a really big assignment.
    C   she hasn't spent time in the library.

22   The lecturer says that reasonable excuses for extensions are

    A   planning problems.
    B   problems with assignment deadlines.
    C   personal illness or accident.

Questions 23–27

What recommendations does Dr Johnson make about the journal articles?

Choose your answers from the box and write the letters A–G next to questions 23–27.

> **A** must read
> **B** useful
> **C** limited value
> **D** read first section
> **E** read research methods
> **F** read conclusion
> **G** don't read

Example	*Answer*
Anderson and Hawker:	**A**

Jackson: **23** ....

Roberts: **24** ....

Morris: **25** ....

Cooper: **26** ....

Forster: **27** ....

Questions 28–30

Label the chart below.

*Choose your answers from the box below and write the letters **A–H** next to questions 28–30.*

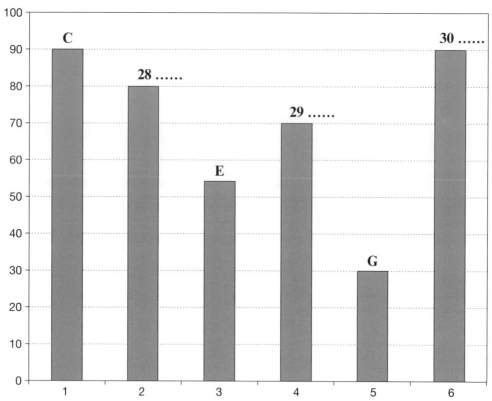

Population studies
Reasons for changing accommodation

	Possible reasons
A	uncooperative landlord
B	environment
C	space
D	noisy neighbours
E	near city
F	work location
G	transport
H	rent

SECTION 4   *Questions 31–40*

Complete the notes below.

*Write **NO MORE THAN TWO WORDS** for each answer.*

THE URBAN LANDSCAPE

Two areas of focus:
- the effect of vegetation on the urban climate
- ways of planning our 31 .... better

Large-scale impact of trees:
- they can make cities more or less 32 ....
- in summer they can make cities cooler
- they can make inland cities more 33 ....

Local impact of trees:
- they can make local areas
  - more 34 ....
  - cooler
  - more humid
  - less windy
  - less 35 ....

<u>Comparing trees and buildings</u>

Temperature regulation:
- trees evaporate water through their 36 ....
- building surfaces may reach high temperatures

Wind force:
- tall buildings cause more wind at 37 .... level
- trees 38 .... the wind force

Noise:
- trees have a small effect on traffic noise
- 39 .... frequency noise passes through trees

Important points to consider:
- trees require a lot of sunlight, water and 40 .... to grow

---

READING

READING PASSAGE 1

*You should spend about 20 minutes on **Questions 1–14** which are based on Reading Passage 1 below.*

Adults and children are frequently confronted with statements about the alarming rate of loss of tropical rainforests. For example, one graphic illustration to which children might readily relate is the estimate that rainforests are being destroyed at a rate equivalent to one thousand football fields every forty minutes – about the duration of a normal classroom period. In the face of the frequent and often vivid media coverage, it is likely that children will have formed ideas about rainforests – what and where they are, why they are important, what endangers them – independent of any formal tuition. It is also possible that some of these ideas will be mistaken.

Many studies have shown that children harbour misconceptions about 'pure', curriculum science. These misconceptions do not remain isolated but become incorporated into a multifaceted, but organised, conceptual framework, making it and the component ideas, some of which are erroneous, more robust but also accessible to modification. These ideas may be developed by children absorbing ideas through the popular media. Sometimes this information may be erroneous. It seems schools may not be providing an opportunity for children to re-express their ideas and so have them tested and refined by teachers and their peers.

Despite the extensive coverage in the popular media of the destruction of rainforests, little formal information is available about children's ideas in this area. The aim of the present study is to start to provide such information, to help teachers design their educational strategies to build upon correct ideas and to displace misconceptions and to plan programmes in environmental studies in their schools.

The study surveys children's scientific knowledge and attitudes to rainforests. Secondary school children were asked to complete a questionnaire containing five open-form questions. The most frequent responses to the first question were descriptions which are self-evident from the term 'rainforest'. Some children described them as damp, wet or hot. The second question concerned the geographical location of rainforests. The commonest responses were continents or countries: Africa (given by 43% of children), South America (30%), Brazil (25%). Some children also gave more general locations, such as being near the Equator.

Responses to question three concerned the importance of rainforests. The dominant idea, raised by 64% of the pupils, was that rainforests provide animals with habitats. Fewer students responded that rainforests provide plant habitats, and even fewer mentioned the indigenous populations of rainforests. More girls (70%) than boys (60%) raised the idea of rainforest as animal habitats.

Similarly, but at a lower level, more girls (13%) than boys (5%) said that rainforests provided human habitats. These observations are generally consistent with our previous studies of pupils' views about the use and conservation of rainforests, in which girls were shown to be more sympathetic to animals and expressed views which seem to place an intrinsic value on non-human animal life.

The fourth question concerned the causes of the destruction of rainforests. Perhaps encouragingly, more than half of the pupils (59%) identified that it is human activities which are destroying rainforests, some personalising the responsibility by the use of terms such as 'we are'. About 18% of the pupils referred specifically to logging activity.

One misconception, expressed by some 10% of the pupils, was that acid rain is responsible for rainforest destruction; a similar proportion said that pollution is destroying rainforests. Here, children are confusing rainforest destruction with damage to the forests of Western Europe by these factors. While two fifths of the students provided the information that the rainforests provide oxygen, in some cases this response also embraced the misconception that rainforest destruction would reduce atmospheric oxygen, making the atmosphere incompatible with human life on Earth.

In answer to the final question about the importance of rainforest conservation, the majority of children simply said that we need rainforests to survive. Only a few of the pupils (6%) mentioned that rainforest destruction may contribute to global warming. This is surprising considering the high level of media coverage on this issue. Some children expressed the idea that the conservation of rainforests is not important.

The results of this study suggest that certain ideas predominate in the thinking of children about rainforests. Pupils' responses indicate some misconceptions in basic scientific knowledge of rainforests' ecosystems such as their ideas about rainforests as habitats for animals, plants and humans and the relationship between climatic change and destruction of rainforests.

Pupils did not volunteer ideas that suggested that they appreciated the complexity of causes of rainforest destruction. In other words, they gave no indication of an appreciation of either the range of ways in which rainforests are important or the complex social, economic and political factors which drive the activities which are destroying the rainforests. One encouragement is that the results of similar studies about other environmental issues suggest that older children seem to acquire the ability to appreciate, value and evaluate conflicting views. Environmental education offers an arena in which these skills can be developed, which is essential for these children as future decision-makers.

Questions 1–8

Do the following statements agree with the information given in Reading Passage 1?

In boxes 1–8 on your answer sheet write

>   **TRUE**   *if the statement agrees with the information*
>   **FALSE**   *if the statement contradicts the information*
>   **NOT GIVEN** *if there is no information on this*

1   The plight of the rainforests has largely been ignored by the media.

2   Children only accept opinions on rainforests that they encounter in their classrooms.

3   It has been suggested that children hold mistaken views about the 'pure' science that they study at school.

4   The fact that children's ideas about science form part of a larger framework of ideas means that it is easier to change them.

5   The study involved asking children a number of yes/no questions such as 'Are there any rainforests in Africa?'

6   Girls are more likely than boys to hold mistaken views about the rainforests' destruction.

7   The study reported here follows on from a series of studies that have looked at children's understanding of rainforests.

8   A second study has been planned to investigate primary school children's ideas about rainforests.

Questions 9–13

The box below gives a list of responses **A–P** to the questionnaire discussed in Reading Passage 1.

Answer the following questions by choosing the correct responses A–P.

Write your answers in boxes 9–13 on your answer sheet.

9   What was the children's most frequent response when asked where the rainforests were?

10   What was the most common response to the question about the importance of the rainforests?

11   What did most children give as the reason for the loss of the rainforests?

12   Why did most children think it important for the rainforests to be protected?

13   Which of the responses is cited as unexpectedly uncommon, given the amount of time spent on the issue by the newspapers and television?

A	There is a complicated combination of reasons for the loss of the rainforests.
B	The rainforests are being destroyed by the same things that are destroying the forests of Western Europe.
C	Rainforests are located near the Equator.
D	Brazil is home to the rainforests.
E	Without rainforests some animals would have nowhere to live.
F	Rainforests are important habitats for a lot of plants.
G	People are responsible for the loss of the rainforests.
H	The rainforests are a source of oxygen.
I	Rainforests are of consequence for a number of different reasons.
J	As the rainforests are destroyed, the world gets warmer.
K	Without rainforests there would not be enough oxygen in the air.
L	There are people for whom the rainforests are home.
M	Rainforests are found in Africa.
N	Rainforests are not really important to human life.
O	The destruction of the rainforests is the direct result of logging activity.
P	Humans depend on the rainforests for their continuing existence.

Question 14

*Choose the correct letter, **A**, **B**, **C**, **D** or **E**.*

Write your answer in box 14 on your answer sheet.

Which of the following is the most suitable title for Reading Passage 1?

    A   The development of a programme in environmental studies within a science curriculum

    B   Children's ideas about the rainforests and the implications for course design

    C   The extent to which children have been misled by the media concerning the rainforests

    D   How to collect, collate and describe the ideas of secondary school children

    E   The importance of the rainforests and the reasons for their destruction

READING PASSAGE 2

*You should spend about 20 minutes on **Questions 15–26** which are based on Reading Passage 2 below.*

What Do Whales Feel?

An examination of the functioning of the senses in cetaceans, the group of mammals comprising whales, dolphins and porpoises

Some of the senses that we and other terrestrial mammals take for granted are either reduced or absent in cetaceans or fail to function well in water. For example, it appears from their brain structure that toothed species are unable to smell. Baleen species, on the other hand, appear to have some related brain structures but it is not known whether these are functional. It has been speculated that, as the blowholes evolved and migrated to the top of the head, the neural pathways serving sense of smell may have been nearly all sacrificed. Similarly, although at least some cetaceans have taste buds, the nerves serving these have degenerated or are rudimentary.

The sense of touch has sometimes been described as weak too, but this view is probably mistaken. Trainers of captive dolphins and small whales often remark on their animals' responsiveness to being touched or rubbed, and both captive and free-ranging cetacean individuals of all species (particularly adults and calves, or members of the same subgroup) appear to make frequent contact. This contact may help to maintain order within a group, and stroking or touching are part of the courtship ritual in most species. The area around the blowhole is also particularly sensitive and captive animals often object strongly to being touched there.

The sense of vision is developed to different degrees in different species. Baleen species studied at close quarters underwater – specifically a grey whale calf in captivity for a year, and free-ranging right whales and humpback whales studied and filmed off Argentina and Hawaii – have obviously tracked objects with vision underwater, and they can apparently see moderately well both in water and in air. However, the position of the eyes so restricts the field of vision in baleen whales that they probably do not have stereoscopic vision.

On the other hand, the position of the eyes in most dolphins and porpoises suggests that they have stereoscopic vision forward and downward. Eye position in freshwater dolphins, which often swim on their side or upside down while feeding, suggests that what vision they have is stereoscopic forward and upward. By comparison, the bottlenose dolphin has extremely keen vision in water. Judging from the way it watches and tracks airborne flying fish, it can apparently see fairly well through the air–water interface as well. And although preliminary experimental evidence suggests that their in-air vision is poor, the accuracy with which dolphins leap high to take small fish out of a trainer's hand provides anecdotal evidence to the contrary.

Such variation can no doubt be explained with reference to the habitats in which individual species have developed. For example, vision is obviously more useful to species inhabiting clear open waters than to those living in turbid rivers and flooded plains. The South American boutu and Chinese beiji, for instance, appear to have very limited vision, and the Indian susus are blind, their eyes reduced to slits that probably allow them to sense only the direction and intensity of light.

Although the senses of taste and smell appear to have deteriorated, and vision in water appears to be uncertain, such weaknesses are more than compensated for by cetaceans' well-developed acoustic sense. Most species are highly vocal, although they vary in the range of sounds they produce, and many forage for food using echolocation[1]. Large baleen whales primarily use the lower frequencies and are often limited in their repertoire. Notable exceptions are the nearly song-like choruses of bowhead whales in summer and the complex, haunting utterances of the humpback whales. Toothed species in general employ more of the frequency spectrum, and produce a wider variety of sounds, than baleen species (though the sperm whale apparently produces a monotonous series of high-energy clicks and little else). Some of the more complicated sounds are clearly communicative, although what role they may play in the social life and 'culture' of cetaceans has been more the subject of wild speculation than of solid science.

---

1. echolocation: the perception of objects by means of sound wave echoes.

Questions 15–21

Complete the table below.

*Choose **NO MORE THAN THREE WORDS** from Reading Passage 2 for each answer.*

Write your answers in boxes 15–21 on your answer sheet.

SENSE	SPECIES	ABILITY	COMMENTS
Smell	toothed	no	evidence from brain structure
	baleen	not certain	related brain structures are present
Taste	some types	poor	nerves linked to their **15**............ are underdeveloped
Touch	all	yes	region around the blowhole very sensitive
Vision	**16**............	yes	probably do not have stereoscopic vision
	dolphins, porpoises	yes	probably have stereoscopic vision **17**............ and ....
	18............	yes	probably have stereoscopic vision forward and upward
	bottlenose dolphin	yes	exceptional in **19**............ and good in air–water interface
	boutu and beiji	poor	have limited vision
	Indian susu	no	probably only sense direction and intensity of light
Hearing	most large baleen	yes	usually use **20**............; repertoire limited
	21............ whales and .... whales	yes	song-like
	toothed	yes	use more of frequency spectrum; have wider repertoire

Questions 22–26

Answer the questions below using **NO MORE THAN THREE WORDS** *from the passage for each answer.*

Write your answers in boxes 22–26 on your answer sheet.

22 Which of the senses is described here as being involved in mating?

23 Which species swims upside down while eating?

24 What can bottlenose dolphins follow from under the water?

25 Which type of habitat is related to good visual ability?

26 Which of the senses is best developed in cetaceans?

READING PASSAGE 3

*You should spend about 20 minutes on **Questions 27–40** which are based on Reading Passage 3 below.*

Visual Symbols and the Blind

Part 1

From a number of recent studies, it has become clear that blind people can appreciate the use of outlines and perspectives to describe the arrangement of objects and other surfaces in space. But pictures are more than literal representations. This fact was drawn to my attention dramatically when a blind woman in one of my investigations decided on her own initiative to draw a wheel as it was spinning. To show this motion, she traced a curve inside the circle (*Fig. 1*). I was taken aback. Lines of motion, such as the one she used, are a very recent invention in the history of illustration. Indeed, as art scholar David Kunzle notes, Wilhelm Busch, a trend-setting nineteenth-century cartoonist, used virtually no motion lines in his popular figures until about 1877.

Fig. 1

When I asked several other blind study subjects to draw a spinning wheel, one particularly clever rendition appeared repeatedly: several subjects showed the wheel's spokes as curved lines. When asked about these curves, they all described them as metaphorical ways of suggesting motion. Majority rule would argue that this device somehow indicated motion very well. But was it a better indicator than, say, broken or wavy lines – or any other kind of line, for that matter? The answer was not clear. So I decided to test whether various lines of motion were apt ways of showing movement or if they were merely idiosyncratic marks. Moreover, I wanted to discover whether there were differences in how the blind and the sighted interpreted lines of motion.

To search out these answers, I created raised-line drawings of five different wheels, depicting spokes with lines that curved, bent, waved, dashed and extended beyond the perimeter of the wheel. I then asked eighteen blind volunteers to feel the wheels and assign one of the following motions to each wheel: wobbling, spinning fast, spinning steadily, jerking or braking. My control group consisted of eighteen sighted undergraduates from the University of Toronto.

All but one of the blind subjects assigned distinctive motions to each wheel. Most guessed that the curved spokes indicated that the wheel was spinning steadily; the wavy spokes, they thought, suggested that the wheel was wobbling; and the bent spokes were taken as a sign that the wheel was jerking. Subjects assumed that spokes extending beyond the wheel's perimeter signified that the wheel had its brakes on and that dashed spokes indicated the wheel was spinning quickly.

In addition, the favoured description for the sighted was the favoured description for the blind in every instance. What is more, the consensus among the sighted was barely higher than that among the blind. Because motion devices are unfamiliar to the blind, the task I gave them involved some problem solving. Evidently, however, the blind not only figured out meanings for each line of motion, but as a group they generally came up with the same meaning at least as frequently as did sighted subjects.

Part 2

We have found that the blind understand other kinds of visual metaphors as well. One blind woman drew a picture of a child inside a heart – choosing that symbol, she said, to show that love surrounded the child. With Chang Hong Liu, a doctoral student from China, I have begun exploring how well blind people understand the symbolism behind shapes such as hearts that do not directly represent their meaning.

We gave a list of twenty pairs of words to sighted subjects and asked them to pick from each pair the term that best related to a circle and the term that best related to a square. For example, we asked: What goes with soft? A circle or a square? Which shape goes with hard?

All our subjects deemed the circle soft and the square hard. A full 94% ascribed happy to the circle, instead of sad. But other pairs revealed less agreement: 79% matched fast to slow and weak to strong, respectively. And only 51% linked deep to circle and shallow to square. (See *Fig. 2*.) When we tested four totally blind volunteers using the same list, we found that their choices closely resembled those made by the sighted subjects. One man, who had been blind since birth, scored extremely well. He made only one match differing from the consensus, assigning 'far' to square and 'near' to circle. In fact, only a small majority of sighted subjects – 53% – had paired far and near to the opposite partners. Thus, we concluded that the blind interpret abstract shapes as sighted people do.

Words associated with circle/square	Agreement among subjects (%)
SOFT-HARD	100
MOTHER-FATHER	94
HAPPY-SAD	94
GOOD-EVIL	89
LOVE-HATE	89
ALIVE-DEAD	87
BRIGHT-DARK	87
LIGHT-HEAVY	85
WARM-COLD	81
SUMMER-WINTER	81
WEAK-STRONG	79
FAST-SLOW	79
CAT-DOG	74
SPRING-FALL	74
QUIET-LOUD	62
WALKING-STANDING	62
ODD-EVEN	57
FAR-NEAR	53
PLANT-ANIMAL	53
DEEP-SHALLOW	51

Fig. 2 Subjects were asked which word in each pair fits best with a circle and which with a square. These percentages show the level of consensus among sighted subjects.

Questions 27–29

*Choose the correct letter, **A**, **B**, **C** or **D**.*

Write your answers in boxes 27–29 on your answer sheet.

27   In the first paragraph the writer makes the point that blind people

    A   may be interested in studying art.
    B   can draw outlines of different objects and surfaces.
    C   can recognise conventions such as perspective.
    D   can draw accurately.

28   The writer was surprised because the blind woman

    A   drew a circle on her own initiative.
    B   did not understand what a wheel looked like.
    C   included a symbol representing movement.
    D   was the first person to use lines of motion.

29   From the experiment described in Part 1, the writer found that the blind subjects

    A   had good understanding of symbols representing movement.
    B   could control the movement of wheels very accurately.
    C   worked together well as a group in solving problems.
    D   got better results than the sighted undergraduates.

Questions 30–32

Look at the following diagrams (Questions 30–32), and the list of types of movement below.

*Match each diagram to the type of movement **A–E** generally assigned to it in the experiment.*

*Choose the correct letter **A–E** and write them in boxes 30–32 on your answer sheet.*

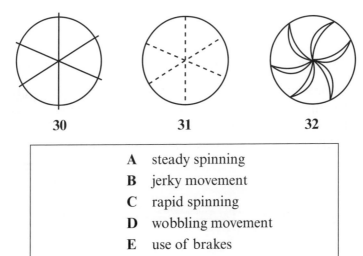

30	**31**	**32**

    A   steady spinning
    B   jerky movement
    C   rapid spinning
    D   wobbling movement
    E   use of brakes

Questions 33–39

Complete the summary below using words from the box.

Write your answers in boxes 33–39 on your answer sheet.

NB You may use any word more than once.

In the experiment described in Part 2, a set of word **33**...... was used to investigate whether blind and sighted people perceived the symbolism in abstract **34**...... in the same way. Subjects were asked which word fitted best with a circle and which with a square. From the **35**...... volunteers, everyone thought a circle fitted 'soft' while a square fitted 'hard'. However, only 51% of the **36**...... volunteers assigned a circle to **37**....... . When the test was later repeated with **38**...... volunteers, it was found that they made **39**...... choices.

associations	blind	deep	hard
hundred	identical	pairs	shapes
sighted	similar	shallow	soft
words			

Question 40

*Choose the correct letter, **A**, **B**, **C** or **D**.*

Write your answer in box 40 on your answer sheet.

Which of the following statements best summarises the writer's general conclusion?

    A   The blind represent some aspects of reality differently from sighted people.
    B   The blind comprehend visual metaphors in similar ways to sighted people.
    C   The blind may create unusual and effective symbols to represent reality.
    D   The blind may be successful artists if given the right training.

WRITING

WRITING TASK 1

You should spend about 20 minutes on this task.

> *The table below shows the proportion of different categories of families living in poverty in Australia in 1999.*
>
> *Summarise the information by selecting and reporting the main features, and make comparisons where relevant.*

Write at least 150 words.

Family type	Proportion of people from each household type living in poverty
single aged person	6% (54,000)
aged couple	4% (48,000)
single, no children	19% (359,000)
couple, no children	7% (211,000)
sole parent	21% (232,000)
couple with children	12% (933,000)
all households	**11% (1,837,000)**

WRITING TASK 2

You should spend about 40 minutes on this task.

Write about the following topic:

> *Compare the advantages and disadvantages of three of the following as media for communicating information. State which you consider to be the most effective.*
>
> - *comics*
> - *books*
> - *radio*
> - *television*
> - *film*
> - *theatre*

Give reasons for your answer and include any relevant examples from your own knowledge or experience.

Write at least 250 words.

SPEAKING

PART 1

The examiner asks the candidate about him/herself, his/her home, work or studies and other familiar topics.

EXAMPLE

Friends

- Are your friends mostly your age or different ages? [Why?]
- Do you usually see your friends during the week or at weekends? [Why?]
- The last time you saw your friends, what did you do together?
- In what ways are your friends important to you?

PART 2

Describe an interesting historic place.
You should say:
   what it is
   where it is located
   what you can see there now
and explain why this place is interesting.

You will have to talk about the topic for one to two minutes.
You have one minute to think about what you're going to say.
You can make some notes to help you if you wish.

PART 3

Discussion topics:

Looking after historic places

Example questions:
How do people in your country feel about protecting historic buildings?
Do you think an area can benefit from having an interesting historic place locally? In what way?
What do you think will happen to historic places or buildings in the future? Why?

The teaching of history at school

Example questions:
How were you taught history when you were at school?
Are there other ways people can learn about history, apart from at school? How?
Do you think history will still be a school subject in the future? Why?

Test 2

SECTION 1   *Questions 1–10*

Questions 1–5

Choose the correct letter, A, B or C.

> *Example*
>
> How long has Sally been waiting?
>
>   **A**   five minutes
>   **B**   twenty minutes
>   **Ⓒ**   thirty minutes

1   What does Peter want to drink?

    A   tea
    B   coffee
    C   a cold drink

2   What caused Peter problems at the bank?

    A   The exchange rate was down.
    B   He was late.
    C   The computers weren't working.

3   Who did Peter talk to at the bank?

    A   an old friend
    B   an American man
    C   a German man

4   Henry gave Peter a map of

    A   the city.
    B   the bus routes.
    C   the train system.

5   What do Peter and Sally decide to order?

    A   food and drinks
    B   just food
    C   just drinks

Questions 6–8

Complete the notes below using words from the box.

Art Gallery
Cathedral
Castle
Gardens
Markets

Tourist attractions open all day: **6** ………………………… and Gardens

Tourist attractions NOT open on Mondays: **7** ………………………… and Castle

Tourist attractions which have free entry: **8** ………………………… and Markets

Questions 9 and 10

Complete the sentences below.

Write NO MORE THAN THREE WORDS for each answer.

 9   The first place Peter and Sally will visit is the…………………………… .

10   At the Cathedral, Peter really wants to …………………………… .

SECTION 2   *Questions 11–20*

Questions 11–20

*Choose the correct letter, **A**, **B** or **C**.*

11   The Counselling Service may contact tutors if

    A   they are too slow in marking assignments.
    B   they give students a lot of work.
    C   they don't inform students about their progress.

12   Stress may be caused by

    A   new teachers.
    B   time pressure.
    C   unfamiliar subject matter.

13   International students may find stress difficult to handle because

    A   they lack support from family and friends.
    B   they don't have time to make new friends.
    C   they find it difficult to socialise.

14   A personal crisis may be caused by

    A   studying for too long overseas.
    B   business problems in the student's own country.
    C   disruptions to personal relationships.

15   Students may lose self-esteem if

    A   they have to change courses.
    B   they don't complete a course.
    C   their family puts too much pressure on them.

16   Students should consult Glenda Roberts if

    A   their general health is poor.
    B   their diet is too strict.
    C   they can't eat the local food.

17   Students in financial difficulties can receive

    A   assistance to buy books.
    B   a loan to pay their course fees.
    C   a no-interest loan to cover study expenses.

18 Loans are also available to students who

    A   can't pay their rent.
    B   need to buy furniture.
    C   can't cover their living expenses.

19 The number of students counselled by the service last year was

    A   214.
    B   240.
    C   2,600.

20 The speaker thinks the Counselling Service

    A   has been effective in spite of staff shortages.
    B   is under-used by students.
    C   has suffered badly because of staff cuts.

SECTION 3   *Questions 21–30*

Questions 21–24

Complete the notes below.

*Write **NO MORE THAN TWO WORDS AND/OR A NUMBER** for each answer.*

DETAILS OF ASSIGNMENT

Part 1   <u>Essay</u>

Title: 'Assess the two main methods of **21** .... in social science research'

Number of words: **22** ....

Part 2   <u>Small-scale study</u>

Choose one method.

Gather data from at least **23** .... subjects.

Part 3   <u>Report on study</u>

Number of words: **24** ....

Questions 25 and 26

*Choose **TWO** letters A–E.*

What **TWO** disadvantages of the questionnaire form of data collection do the students discuss?

    A   The data is sometimes invalid.
    B   Too few people may respond.
    C   It is less likely to reveal the unexpected.
    D   It can only be used with literate populations.
    E   There is a delay between the distribution and return of questionnaires.

Questions 27–30

Complete the table below.

Write **NO MORE THAN THREE WORDS OR A NUMBER** *for each answer.*

AUTHOR	TITLE	PUBLISHER	YEAR OF PUBLICATION
27	'Sample Surveys in Social Science Research'		
Bell	**28**	**29**	
Wilson	'Interviews that work'	Oxford University Press	**30** ....

SECTION 4   *Questions 31–40*

Questions 31 and 32

*Choose the correct letter, **A**, **B** or **C**.*

31   Corporate crime is generally committed

    A   against individuals.
    B   by groups.
    C   for companies.

32   Corporate crime does **NOT** include

    A   employees stealing from their company.
    B   unintentional crime by employees.
    C   fraud resulting from company policy.

Questions 33–38

Complete the notes below.

*Write **NO MORE THAN THREE WORDS** for each answer.*

Corporate crime has been ignored by:
    a)   the **33** .... e.g. films
    b)   **34** ....

Reasons:
    a)   often more complex, and needing **35** ....
    b)   less human interest than conventional crime
    c)   victims often **36** ....

Effects:
    a)   Economic costs
       • may appear unimportant to **37** ....
       • can make large **38** .... for company
       • cause more losses to individuals than conventional crimes
    b)   Social costs
       • make people lose trust in business world
       • affect poorer people most

Questions 39 and 40

Choose **TWO** *letters A–F.*

The oil tanker explosion was an example of a crime which

    A   was no-one's fault.
    B   was not a corporate crime.
    C   was intentional.
    D   was caused by indifference.
    E   had tragic results.
    F   made a large profit for the company.

READING

READING PASSAGE 1

*You should spend about 20 minutes on **Questions 1–13** which are based on Reading Passage 1 below.*

Lost for Words

Many minority languages are on the danger list

In the Native American Navajo nation, which sprawls across four states in the American south-west, the native language is dying. Most of its speakers are middle-aged or elderly. Although many students take classes in Navajo, the schools are run in English. Street signs, supermarket goods and even their own newspaper are all in English. Not surprisingly, linguists doubt that any native speakers of Navajo will remain in a hundred years' time.

Navajo is far from alone. Half the world's 6,800 languages are likely to vanish within two generations – that's one language lost every ten days. Never before has the planet's linguistic diversity shrunk at such a pace. 'At the moment, we are heading for about three or four languages dominating the world,' says Mark Pagel, an evolutionary biologist at the University of Reading. 'It's a mass extinction, and whether we will ever rebound from the loss is difficult to know.'

Isolation breeds linguistic diversity: as a result, the world is peppered with languages spoken by only a few people. Only 250 languages have more than a million speakers, and at least 3,000 have fewer than 2,500. It is not necessarily these small languages that are about to disappear. Navajo is considered endangered despite having 150,000 speakers. What makes a language endangered is not just the number of speakers, but how old they are. If it is spoken by children it is relatively safe. The critically endangered languages are those that are only spoken by the elderly, according to Michael Krauss, director of the Alassk Native Language Center, in Fairbanks.

Why do people reject the language of their parents? It begins with a crisis of confidence, when a small community finds itself alongside a larger, wealthier society, says Nicholas Ostler, of Britain's Foundation for Endangered Languages, in Bath. 'People lose faith in their culture,' he says. 'When the next generation reaches their teens, they might not want to be induced into the old traditions.'

The change is not always voluntary. Quite often, governments try to kill off a minority language by banning its use in public or discouraging its use in schools, all to promote national unity.

The former US policy of running Indian reservation schools in English, for example, effectively put languages such as Navajo on the danger list. But Salikoko Mufwene, who chairs the Linguistics department at the University of Chicago, argues that the deadliest weapon is not government policy but economic globalisation. 'Native Americans have not lost pride in their language, but they have had to adapt to socio-economic pressures,' he says. 'They cannot refuse to speak English if most commercial activity is in English.' But are languages worth saving? At the very least, there is a loss of data for the study of languages and their evolution, which relies on comparisons between languages, both living and dead. When an unwritten and unrecorded language disappears, it is lost to science.

Language is also intimately bound up with culture, so it may be difficult to preserve one without the other. 'If a person shifts from Navajo to English, they lose something,' Mufwene says. 'Moreover, the loss of diversity may also deprive us of different ways of looking at the world,' says Pagel. There is mounting evidence that learning a language produces physiological changes in the brain. 'Your brain and mine are different from the brain of someone who speaks French, for instance,' Pagel says, and this could affect our thoughts and perceptions. 'The patterns and connections we make among various concepts may be structured by the linguistic habits of our community.'

So despite linguists' best efforts, many languages will disappear over the next century. But a growing interest in cultural identity may prevent the direst predictions from coming true. 'The key to fostering diversity is for people to learn their ancestral tongue, as well as the dominant language,' says Doug Whalen, founder and president of the Endangered Language Fund in New Haven, Connecticut. 'Most of these languages will not survive without a large degree of bilingualism,' he says. In New Zealand, classes for children have slowed the erosion of Maori and rekindled interest in the language. A similar approach in Hawaii has produced about 8,000 new speakers of Polynesian languages in the past few years. In California, 'apprentice' programmes have provided life support to several indigenous languages. Volunteer 'apprentices' pair up with one of the last living speakers of a Native American tongue to learn a traditional skill such as basket weaving, with instruction exclusively in the endangered language. After about 300 hours of training they are generally sufficiently fluent to transmit the language to the next generation. But Mufwene says that preventing a language dying out is not the same as giving it new life by using it every day. 'Preserving a language is more like preserving fruits in a jar,' he says.

However, preservation can bring a language back from the dead. There are examples of languages that have survived in written form and then been revived by later generations. But a written form is essential for this, so the mere possibility of revival has led many speakers of endangered languages to develop systems of writing where none existed before.

Questions 1–4

Complete the summary below.

*Choose **NO MORE THAN TWO WORDS** from the passage for each answer.*

Write your answers in boxes 1–4 on your answer sheet.

There are currently approximately 6,800 languages in the world. This great variety of languages came about largely as a result of geographical **1**…… . But in today's world, factors such as government initiatives and **2**…… are contributing to a huge decrease in the number of languages. One factor which may help to ensure that some endangered languages do not die out completely is people's increasing appreciation of their **3**…… . This has been encouraged through programmes of language classes for children and through 'apprentice' schemes, in which the endangered language is used as the medium of instruction to teach people a **4**…… . Some speakers of endangered languages have even produced writing systems in order to help secure the survival of their mother tongue.

Questions 5–9

Look at the following statements (Questions 5–9) and the list of people in the box below.

Match each statement with the correct person A–E.

Write the appropriate letter A–E in boxes 5–9 on your answer sheet.

NB You may use any letter more than once.

5 Endangered languages cannot be saved unless people learn to speak more than one language.

6 Saving languages from extinction is not in itself a satisfactory goal.

7 The way we think may be determined by our language.

8 Young people often reject the established way of life in their community.

9 A change of language may mean a loss of traditional culture.

A	Michael Krauss
B	Salikoko Mufwene
C	Nicholas Ostler
D	Mark Pagel
E	Doug Whalen

Questions 10–13

Do the following statements agree with the views of the writer in Reading Passage 1?

In boxes 10–13 on your answer sheet write

> **YES**   *if the statement agrees with the views of the writer*
> **NO**   *if the statement contradicts the views of the writer*
> **NOT GIVEN** *if it is impossible to say what the writer thinks about this*

10   The Navajo language will die out because it currently has too few speakers.

11   A large number of native speakers fails to guarantee the survival of a language.

12   National governments could do more to protect endangered languages.

13   The loss of linguistic diversity is inevitable.

READING PASSAGE 2

*You should spend about 20 minutes on **Questions 14–26** which are based on Reading Passage 2 below.*

ALTERNATIVE MEDICINE IN AUSTRALIA

The first students to study alternative medicine at university level in Australia began their four-year, full-time course at the University of Technology, Sydney, in early 1994. Their course covered, among other therapies, acupuncture. The theory they learnt is based on the traditional Chinese explanation of this ancient healing art: that it can regulate the flow of 'Qi' or energy through pathways in the body. This course reflects how far some alternative therapies have come in their struggle for acceptance by the medical establishment.

Australia has been unusual in the Western world in having a very conservative attitude to natural or alternative therapies, according to Dr Paul Laver, a lecturer in Public Health at the University of Sydney. 'We've had a tradition of doctors being fairly powerful and I guess they are pretty loath to allow any pretenders to their position to come into it.' In many other industrialised countries, orthodox and alternative medicine have worked 'hand in glove' for years. In Europe, only orthodox doctors can prescribe herbal medicine. In Germany, plant remedies account for 10% of the national turnover of pharmaceuticals. Americans made more visits to alternative therapists than to orthodox doctors in 1990, and each year they spend about $US12 billion on therapies that have not been scientifically tested.

Disenchantment with orthodox medicine has seen the popularity of alternative therapies in Australia climb steadily during the past 20 years. In a 1983 national health survey, 1.9% of people said they had contacted a chiropractor, naturopath, osteopath, acupuncturist or herbalist in the two weeks prior to the survey. By 1990, this figure had risen to 2.6% of the population. The 550,000 consultations with alternative therapists reported in the 1990 survey represented about an eighth of the total number of consultations with medically qualified personnel covered by the survey, according to Dr Laver and colleagues writing in the *Australian Journal of Public Health* in 1993. 'A better educated and less accepting public has become disillusioned with the experts in general, and increasingly sceptical about science and empirically based knowledge,' they said. 'The high standing of professionals, including doctors, has been eroded as a consequence.'

Rather than resisting or criticising this trend, increasing numbers of Australian doctors, particularly younger ones, are forming group practices with alternative therapists or taking courses themselves, particularly in acupuncture and herbalism. Part of the incentive was financial, Dr Laver said. 'The bottom line is that most general practitioners are business people. If they see potential clientele going elsewhere, they might want to be able to offer a similar service.'

In 1993, Dr Laver and his colleagues published a survey of 289 Sydney people who attended eight alternative therapists' practices in Sydney. These practices offered a wide range of alternative therapies from 25 therapists. Those surveyed had experienced chronic illnesses, for which orthodox medicine had been able to provide little relief. They commented that they liked the holistic approach of their alternative therapists and the friendly, concerned and detailed attention they had received. The cold, impersonal manner of orthodox doctors featured in the survey. An increasing exodus from their clinics, coupled with this and a number of other relevant surveys carried out in Australia, all pointing to orthodox doctors' inadequacies, have led mainstream doctors themselves to begin to admit they could learn from the personal style of alternative therapists. Dr Patrick Store, President of the Royal College of General Practitioners, concurs that orthodox doctors could learn a lot about bedside manner and advising patients on preventative health from alternative therapists.

According to the *Australian Journal of Public Health*, 18% of patients visiting alternative therapists do so because they suffer from musculo-skeletal complaints; 12% suffer from digestive problems, which is only 1% more than those suffering from emotional problems. Those suffering from respiratory complaints represent 7% of their patients, and candida sufferers represent an equal percentage. Headache sufferers and those complaining of general ill health represent 6% and 5% of patients respectively, and a further 4% see therapists for general health maintenance.

The survey suggested that complementary medicine is probably a better term than alternative medicine. Alternative medicine appears to be an adjunct, sought in times of disenchantment when conventional medicine seems not to offer the answer.

Questions 14 and 15

*Choose the correct letter, **A**, **B**, **C** or **D**.*

Write your answers in boxes 14 and 15 on your answer sheet.

14   Traditionally, how have Australian doctors differed from doctors in many Western countries?

   A   They have worked closely with pharmaceutical companies.
   B   They have often worked alongside other therapists.
   C   They have been reluctant to accept alternative therapists.
   D   They have regularly prescribed alternative remedies.

15   In 1990, Americans

   A   were prescribed more herbal medicines than in previous years.
   B   consulted alternative therapists more often than doctors.
   C   spent more on natural therapies than orthodox medicines.
   D   made more complaints about doctors than in previous years.

Questions 16–23

Do the following statements agree with the views of the writer in Reading Passage 2?

In boxes 16–23 on your answer sheet write

> **YES**   *if the statement agrees with the views of the writer*
> **NO**   *if the statement contradicts the views of the writer*
> **NOT GIVEN**   *if it is impossible to say what the writer thinks about this*

16   Australians have been turning to alternative therapies in increasing numbers over the past 20 years.

17   Between 1983 and 1990 the numbers of patients visiting alternative therapists rose to include a further 8% of the population.

18   The 1990 survey related to 550,000 consultations with alternative therapists.

19   In the past, Australians had a higher opinion of doctors than they do today.

20   Some Australian doctors are retraining in alternative therapies.

21   Alternative therapists earn higher salaries than doctors.

22   The 1993 Sydney survey involved 289 patients who visited alternative therapists for acupuncture treatment.

23   All the patients in the 1993 Sydney survey had long-term medical complaints.

Questions 24–26

Complete the vertical axis on the table below.

*Choose **NO MORE THAN THREE WORDS** from Reading Passage 2 for each answer.*

Write your answers in boxes 24–26 on your answer sheet.

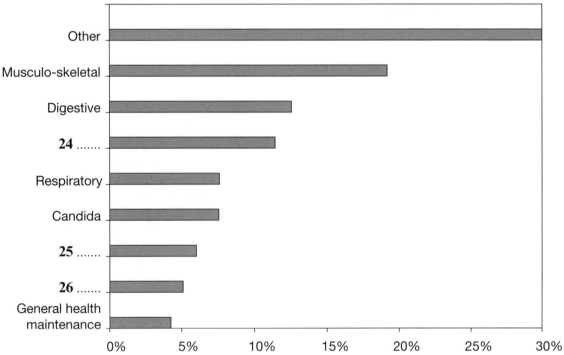

Medical complaints of patients visiting therapists

READING PASSAGE 3

*You should spend about 20 minutes on **Questions 27–40** which are based on Reading Passage 3 below.*

PLAY IS A SERIOUS BUSINESS

Does play help develop bigger, better brains?
Bryant Furlow investigates

A Playing is a serious business. Children engrossed in a make-believe world, fox cubs play-fighting or kittens teasing a ball of string aren't just having fun. Play may look like a carefree and exuberant way to pass the time before the hard work of adulthood comes along, but there's much more to it than that. For a start, play can even cost animals their lives. Eighty per cent of deaths among juvenile fur seals occur because playing pups fail to spot predators approaching. It is also extremely expensive in terms of energy. Playful young animals use around two or three per cent of their energy cavorting, and in children that figure can be closer to fifteen per cent. 'Even two or three per cent is huge,' says John Byers of Idaho University. 'You just don't find animals wasting energy like that,' he adds. There must be a reason.

B But if play is not simply a developmental hiccup, as biologists once thought, why did it evolve? The latest idea suggests that play has evolved to build big brains. In other words, playing makes you intelligent. Playfulness, it seems, is common only among mammals, although a few of the larger-brained birds also indulge. Animals at play often use unique signs – tail-wagging in dogs, for example – to indicate that activity superficially resembling adult behaviour is not really in earnest. A popular explanation of play has been that it helps juveniles develop the skills they will need to hunt, mate and socialise as adults. Another has been that it allows young animals to get in shape for adult life by improving their respiratory endurance. Both these ideas have been questioned in recent years.

C Take the exercise theory. If play evolved to build muscle or as a kind of endurance training, then you would expect to see permanent benefits. But Byers points out that the benefits of increased exercise disappear rapidly after training stops, so any improvement in endurance resulting from juvenile play would be lost by adulthood. 'If the function of play was to get into shape,' says Byers, 'the optimum time for playing would depend on when it was most advantageous for the young of a particular species to do so. But it doesn't work like that.' Across species, play tends to peak about halfway through the suckling stage and then decline.

D Then there's the skills-training hypothesis. At first glance, playing animals do appear to be practising the complex manoeuvres they will need in adulthood. But a closer inspection reveals this interpretation as too simplistic. In one study, behavioural ecologist Tim Caro, from the University of California, looked at the predatory play of kittens and their predatory behaviour when they reached adulthood. He found that the way the cats played had no significant effect on their hunting prowess in later life.

E Earlier this year, Sergio Pellis of Lethbridge University, Canada, reported that there is a strong positive link between brain size and playfulness among mammals in general. Comparing measurements for fifteen orders of mammal, he and his team found larger brains (for a given body size) are linked to greater playfulness. The converse was also found to be true. Robert Barton of Durham University believes that, because large brains are more sensitive to developmental stimuli than smaller brains, they require more play to help mould them for adulthood. 'I concluded it's to do with learning, and with the importance of environmental data to the brain during development,' he says.

F According to Byers, the timing of the playful stage in young animals provides an important clue to what's going on. If you plot the amount of time a juvenile devotes to play each day over the course of its development, you discover a pattern typically associated with a 'sensitive period' – a brief development window during which the brain can actually be modified in ways that are not possible earlier or later in life. Think of the relative ease with which young children – but not infants or adults – absorb language. Other researchers have found that play in cats, rats and mice is at its most intense just as this 'window of opportunity' reaches its peak.

G 'People have not paid enough attention to the amount of the brain activated by play,' says Marc Bekoff from Colorado University. Bekoff studied coyote pups at play and found that the kind of behaviour involved was markedly more variable and unpredictable than that of adults. Such behaviour activates many different parts of the brain, he reasons. Bekoff likens it to a behavioural kaleidoscope, with animals at play jumping rapidly between activities. 'They use behaviour from a lot of different contexts – predation, aggression, reproduction,' he says. 'Their developing brain is getting all sorts of stimulation.'

H Not only is more of the brain involved in play than was suspected, but it also seems to activate higher cognitive processes. 'There's enormous cognitive involvement in play,' says Bekoff. He points out that play often involves complex assessments of playmates, ideas of reciprocity and the use of specialised signals and rules. He believes that play creates a brain that has greater behavioural flexibility and improved potential for learning later in life. The idea is backed up by the work of Stephen Siviy of Gettysburg College. Siviy studied how bouts of play affected the brain's levels of a particular chemical associated with the stimulation and growth of nerve cells. He was surprised by the extent of the activation. 'Play just lights everything up,' he says. By allowing link-ups between brain areas that might not normally communicate with each other, play may enhance creativity.

I What might further experimentation suggest about the way children are raised in many societies today? We already know that rat pups denied the chance to play grow smaller brain components and fail to develop the ability to apply social rules when they interact with their peers. With schooling beginning earlier and becoming increasingly exam-orientated, play is likely to get even less of a look-in. Who knows what the result of that will be?

Questions 27–32

Reading Passage 3 has nine paragraphs labelled **A–I**.

Which paragraph contains the following information?

*Write the correct letter **A–I** in boxes 27–32 on your answer sheet.*

NB *You may use any letter more than once.*

27 the way play causes unusual connections in the brain which are beneficial

28 insights from recording how much time young animals spend playing

29 a description of the physical hazards that can accompany play

30 a description of the mental activities which are exercised and developed during play

31 the possible effects that a reduction in play opportunities will have on humans

32 the classes of animals for which play is important

Questions 33–35

*Choose **THREE** letters A–F.*

Write your answers in boxes 33–35 on your answer sheet.

The list below gives some ways of regarding play.

Which **THREE** ways are mentioned by the writer of the text?

    A   a rehearsal for later adult activities
    B   a method animals use to prove themselves to their peer group
    C   an activity intended to build up strength for adulthoood
    D   a means of communicating feelings
    E   a defensive strategy
    F   an activity assisting organ growth

Questions 36–40

Look at the following researchers (Questions 36–40) and the list of findings below.

Match each researcher with the correct finding.

*Write the correct letter **A–H** in boxes 36–40 on your answer sheet.*

36   Robert Barton

37   Marc Bekoff

38   John Byers

39   Sergio Pellis

40   Stephen Siviy

List of Findings

A   There is a link between a specific substance in the brain and playing.

B   Play provides input concerning physical surroundings.

C   Varieties of play can be matched to different stages of evolutionary history.

D   There is a tendency for mammals with smaller brains to play less.

E   Play is not a form of fitness training for the future.

F   Some species of larger-brained birds engage in play.

G   A wide range of activities are combined during play.

H   Play is a method of teaching survival techniques.

WRITING

WRITING TASK 1

You should spend about 20 minutes on this task.

> *The graph below shows the demand for electricity in England during typical days in winter and summer. The pie chart shows how electricity is used in an average English home.*
>
> *Summarise the information by selecting and reporting the main features, and make comparisons where relevant.*

Write at least 150 words.

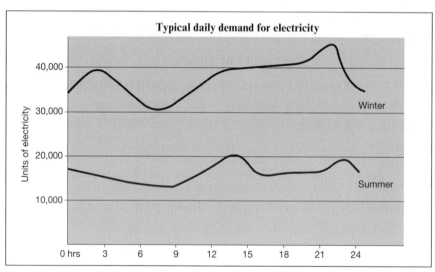

Typical daily demand for electricity

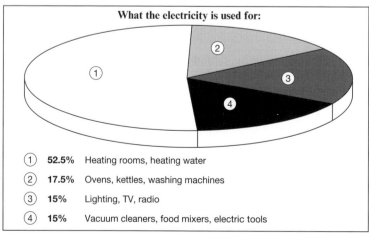

What the electricity is used for:

①	**52.5%**	Heating rooms, heating water
②	**17.5%**	Ovens, kettles, washing machines
③	**15%**	Lighting, TV, radio
④	**15%**	Vacuum cleaners, food mixers, electric tools

WRITING TASK 2

You should spend about 40 minutes on this task.

Write about the following topic:

>   ***Happiness is considered very important in life.***
>
>   ***Why is it difficult to define?***
>
>   ***What factors are important in achieving happiness?***

Give reasons for your answer and include any relevant examples from your own knowledge or experience.

Write at least 250 words.

SPEAKING

PART 1

The examiner asks the candidate about him/herself, his/her home, work or studies and other familiar topics.

EXAMPLE

Food and cooking

- What kinds of food do you like to eat?
- What kind of new food would you like to try? [Why?]
- Do you like cooking? [Why/Why not?]
- What was the last meal you cooked?
- Do you prefer home-cooked food or food from restaurants? [Why?]

PART 2

Describe an interest or hobby that you enjoy.
You should say:
   how you became interested in it
   how long you have been doing it
   why you enjoy it
and explain what benefits you get from this interest or hobby.

You will have to talk about the topic for one to two minutes.
You have one minute to think about what you're going to say.
You can make some notes to help you if you wish.

PART 3

Discussion topics:

The social benefits of hobbies

Example questions:
Do you think having a hobby is good for people's social life? In what way?
Are there any negative effects of a person spending too much time on their hobby? What are they?
Why do you think people need to have an interest or hobby?

Leisure time

Example questions:
In your country, how much time do people spend on work and how much time on leisure? Is this a good balance, do you think?
Would you say the amount of free time has changed much in the last fifty years?
Do you think people will have more or less free time in the future? Why?

Test 3

SECTION 1   *Questions 1–10*

Questions 1–4

Complete the form below.

*Write **NO MORE THAN THREE WORDS AND/OR NUMBERS** for each answer.*

Accommodation Request Form

Example	*Answer*
Name:	*Sara Lim*
	. . . .

Age: 23

Length of time in Australia: 1 . . . .

Present address: Flat 1,
539, 2 . . . . Road
Canterbury 2036

Present course: 3 . . . . English

Accommodation required from: 4 . . . . ,
7th September

Questions 5–7

*Choose the correct letter, **A**, **B** or **C**.*

5   Sara requires a

    A   single room.
    B   twin room.
    C   triple room.

6   She would prefer to live with a

    A   family.
    B   single person.
    C   couple.

7   She would like to live in a

    A   flat.
    B   house.
    C   studio apartment.

Questions 8–10

Complete the sentences below.

*Write **NO MORE THAN ONE WORD** for each answer.*

8   The .... will be \$320.

9   She needs to pay the rent by cash or cheque on a .... basis.

10   She needs to pay her part of the .... bill.

SECTION 2   *Questions 11–20*

Questions 11–14

*Choose the correct letter, **A**, **B** or **C**.*

11   When is this year's festival being held?

A   1–13 January
B   5–17 January
C   25–31 January

12   What will the reviewer concentrate on today?

A   theatre
B   dance
C   exhibitions

13   How many circuses are there in the festival?

A   one
B   two
C   several

14   Where does Circus Romano perform?

A   in a theatre
B   in a tent
C   in a stadium

Questions 15–20

Complete the notes below.

*Write **NO MORE THAN THREE WORDS** for each answer.*

	Where	Type of performance	Highlights	Type of audience
Circus Romano		Clowns and acrobats	Music and 15	16 ....
Circus Electrica	17	Dancers and magicians	Aerial displays	18 ....
Mekong Water Puppets	19	Puppets	Seeing the puppeteers at the end	20 ....

SECTION 3   *Questions 21–30*

Questions 21–25

*Choose the correct letter, **A**, **B** or **C**.*

21   The man wants information on courses for

   A   people going back to college.
   B   postgraduate students.
   C   business executives.

22   The 'Study for Success' seminar lasts for

   A   one day.
   B   two days.
   C   three days.

23   In the seminar the work on writing aims to improve

   A   confidence.
   B   speed.
   C   clarity.

24   Reading sessions help students to read

   A   analytically.
   B   as fast as possible.
   C   thoroughly.

25   The seminar tries to

   A   prepare learners physically.
   B   encourage interest in learning.
   C   develop literacy skills.

Questions 26–30

*Choose the correct letter, **A**, **B** or **C**.*

26 A key component of the course is learning how to

   A   use time effectively.
   B   stay healthy.
   C   select appropriate materials.

27 Students who want to do the 'Study for Success' seminar should

   A   register with the Faculty Office.
   B   contact their Course Convenor.
   C   reserve a place in advance.

28 The 'Learning Skills for University Study' course takes place on

   A   Monday, Wednesday and Friday.
   B   Monday, Tuesday and Wednesday.
   C   Monday, Thursday and Friday.

29 A feature of this course is

   A   a physical training component.
   B   advice on coping with stress.
   C   a detailed weekly planner.

30 The man chooses the 'Study for Success' seminar because

   A   he is over forty.
   B   he wants to start at the beginning.
   C   he seeks to revise his skills.

SECTION 4   *Questions 31–40*

Questions 31 and 32

Complete the notes below.

*Write **NO MORE THAN TWO WORDS AND/OR A NUMBER** for each answer.*

New Union Building

Procedures to establish student opinion:

• students were asked to give written suggestions on the building's design

• these points informed the design of a 31 ....
  (there were 32 .... respondents)

• results collated and report produced by Union Committee

Questions 33–37

Complete the table below.

*Write **NO MORE THAN THREE WORDS** for each answer.*

CHOICE OF SITE			
	Site One	**Site Two**	**Site Three**
Location	City centre near Faculty of 33	Outskirts near park	Out of town near the 34 ....
Advantages and/or disadvantages	Problems with 35 .... and	Close to 36	Access to living quarters. Larger site, so more 37 ....

Question 38

*Choose **TWO** letters A–G.*

Which **TWO** facilities did the students request in the new Union building?

    A   a library
    B   a games room
    C   a student health centre
    D   a mini fitness centre
    E   a large swimming pool
    F   a travel agency
    G   a lecture theatre

Question 39

*Choose the correct letter, **A**, **B** or **C**.*

Which argument was used **AGAINST** having a drama theatre?

    A   It would be expensive and no students would use it.
    B   It would be a poor use of resources because only a minority would use it.
    C   It could not accommodate large productions of plays.

Question 40

*Choose **TWO** letters A–E.*

Which **TWO** security measures have been requested?

    A   closed-circuit TV
    B   show Union Card on entering the building
    C   show Union Card when asked
    D   spot searches of bags
    E   permanent Security Office on site

READING

READING PASSAGE 1

*You should spend about 20 minutes on **Questions 1–13** which are based on Reading Passage 1 below.*

Micro-Enterprise Credit for Street Youth

> *'I am from a large, poor family and for many years we have done without breakfast. Ever since I joined the Street Kids International program I have been able to buy my family sugar and buns for breakfast. I have also bought myself decent second-hand clothes and shoes.'*
> Doreen Soko
>
> *'We've had business experience. Now I'm confident to expand what we've been doing. I've learnt cash management, and the way of keeping money so we save for re-investment. Now business is a part of our lives. As well, we didn't know each other before – now we've made new friends.'*
> Fan Kaoma
>
> **Participants in the Youth Skills Enterprise Initiative Program, Zambia**

Introduction

Although small-scale business training and credit programs have become more common throughout the world, relatively little attention has been paid to the need to direct such opportunities to young people. Even less attention has been paid to children living on the street or in difficult circumstances.

Over the past nine years, Street Kids International (S.K.I.) has been working with partner organisations in Africa, Latin America and India to support the economic lives of street children. The purpose of this paper is to share some of the lessons S.K.I. and our partners have learned.

Background

Typically, children do not end up on the streets due to a single cause, but to a combination of factors: a dearth of adequately funded schools, the demand for income at home, family breakdown and violence. The street may be attractive to children as a place to find adventurous play and money. However, it is also a place where some children are exposed, with little or no protection, to exploitative employment, urban crime, and abuse.

Children who work on the streets are generally involved in unskilled, labour-intensive tasks which require long hours, such as shining shoes, carrying goods, guarding or washing cars, and informal trading. Some may also earn income through begging, or through theft and other illegal activities. At the same time, there are street children who take pride in supporting themselves and their families and who often enjoy their work. Many children may choose entrepreneurship because it allows them a degree of independence, is less exploitative than many forms of paid employment, and is flexible enough to allow them to participate in other activities such as education and domestic tasks.

Street Business Partnerships

S.K.I. has worked with partner organisations in Latin America, Africa and India to develop innovative opportunities for street children to earn income.

- The S.K.I. Bicycle Courier Service first started in the Sudan. Participants in this enterprise were supplied with bicycles, which they used to deliver parcels and messages, and which they were required to pay for gradually from their wages. A similar program was taken up in Bangalore, India.
- Another successful project, The Shoe Shine Collective, was a partnership program with the Y.W.C.A. in the Dominican Republic. In this project, participants were lent money to purchase shoe shine boxes. They were also given a safe place to store their equipment, and facilities for individual savings plans.
- The Youth Skills Enterprise Initiative in Zambia is a joint program with the Red Cross Society and the Y.W.C.A. Street youths are supported to start their own small business through business training, life skills training and access to credit.

Lessons learned

The following lessons have emerged from the programs that S.K.I. and partner organisations have created.

- Being an entrepreneur is not for everyone, nor for every street child. Ideally, potential participants will have been involved in the organisation's programs for at least six months, and trust and relationship-building will have already been established.
- The involvement of the participants has been essential to the development of relevant programs. When children have had a major role in determining procedures, they are more likely to abide by and enforce them.
- It is critical for all loans to be linked to training programs that include the development of basic business and life skills.
- There are tremendous advantages to involving parents or guardians in the program, where such relationships exist. Home visits allow staff the opportunity to know where the participants live, and to understand more about each individual's situation.
- Small loans are provided initially for purchasing fixed assets such as bicycles, shoe shine kits and basic building materials for a market stall. As the entrepreneurs gain experience, the enterprises can be gradually expanded and consideration can be given to increasing loan amounts. The loan amounts in S.K.I. programs have generally ranged from US$30–$100.
- All S.K.I. programs have charged interest on the loans, primarily to get the entrepreneurs used to the concept of paying interest on borrowed money. Generally the rates have been modest (lower than bank rates).

Conclusion

There is a need to recognise the importance of access to credit for impoverished young people seeking to fulfil economic needs. The provision of small loans to support the entrepreneurial dreams and ambitions of youth can be an effective means to help them change their lives. However, we believe that credit must be extended in association with other types of support that help participants develop critical life skills as well as productive businesses.

Questions 1–4

*Choose the correct letter, **A**, **B**, **C** or **D**.*

Write your answers in boxes 1–4 on your answer sheet.

1   The quotations in the box at the beginning of the article

    A   exemplify the effects of S.K.I.
    B   explain why S.K.I. was set up.
    C   outline the problems of street children.
    D   highlight the benefits to society of S.K.I.

2   The main purpose of S.K.I. is to

    A   draw the attention of governments to the problem of street children.
    B   provide schools and social support for street children.
    C   encourage the public to give money to street children.
    D   give business training and loans to street children.

3   Which of the following is mentioned by the writer as a reason why children end up living on the streets?

    A   unemployment
    B   war
    C   poverty
    D   crime

4   In order to become more independent, street children may

    A   reject paid employment.
    B   leave their families.
    C   set up their own businesses.
    D   employ other children.

Questions 5–8

Complete the table below.

*Choose **NO MORE THAN THREE WORDS** from Reading Passage 1 for each answer.*

Write your answers in boxes 5–8 on your answer sheet.

Country	Organisations Involved	Type of Project	Support Provided
5 .... and	• S.K.I.	courier service	• provision of 6 ....
Dominican Republic	• S.K.I. • Y.W.C.A.	7	• loans • storage facilities • savings plans
Zambia	• S.K.I. • The Red Cross • Y.W.C.A.	setting up small businesses	• business training • 8 .... training • access to credit

Questions 9–12

Do the following statements agree with the claims of the writer in Reading Passage 1?

In boxes 9–12 on your answer sheet write

> **YES** *if the statement agrees with the claims of the writer*
> **NO** *if the statement contradicts the claims of the writer*
> **NOT GIVEN** *if it is impossible to say what the writer thinks about this*

9   Any street child can set up their own small business if given enough support.

10   In some cases, the families of street children may need financial support from S.K.I.

11   Only one fixed loan should be given to each child.

12   The children have to pay back slightly more money than they borrowed.

Question 13

*Choose the correct letter, **A**, **B**, **C** or **D**.*

Write your answer in box 13 on your answer sheet.

The writers conclude that money should only be lent to street children

> **A**   as part of a wider program of aid.
> **B**   for programs that are not too ambitious.
> **C**   when programs are supported by local businesses.
> **D**   if the projects planned are realistic and useful.

READING PASSAGE 2

*You should spend about 20 minutes on **Questions 14–26** which are based on Reading Passage 2 on the following pages.*

Questions 14–17

Reading Passage 2 has four sections **A–D**.

Choose the correct heading for each section from the list of headings below.

*Write the correct number **i–vi** in boxes 14–17 on your answer sheet.*

List of Headings
i   Causes of volcanic eruption
ii   Efforts to predict volcanic eruption
iii Volcanoes and the features of our planet
iv   Different types of volcanic eruption
v   International relief efforts
vi   The unpredictability of volcanic eruptions

14   Section **A**

15   Section **B**

16   Section **C**

17   Section **D**

Volcanoes – earth-shattering news

When Mount Pinatubo suddenly erupted on 9 June 1991, the power of volcanoes past and present again hit the headlines

A Volcanoes are the ultimate earth-moving machinery. A violent eruption can blow the top few kilometres off a mountain, scatter fine ash practically all over the globe and hurl rock fragments into the stratosphere to darken the skies a continent away.

But the classic eruption – cone-shaped mountain, big bang, mushroom cloud and surges of molten lava – is only a tiny part of a global story. Vulcanism, the name given to volcanic processes, really has shaped the world. Eruptions have rifted continents, raised mountain chains, constructed islands and shaped the topography of the earth. The entire ocean floor has a basement of volcanic basalt.

Volcanoes have not only made the continents, they are also thought to have made the world's first stable atmosphere and provided all the water for the oceans, rivers and ice-caps. There are now about 600 active volcanoes. Every year they add two or three cubic kilometres of rock to the continents. Imagine a similar number of volcanoes smoking away for the last 3,500 million years. That is enough rock to explain the continental crust.

What comes out of volcanic craters is mostly gas. More than 90% of this gas is water vapour from the deep earth: enough to explain, over 3,500 million years, the water in the oceans. The rest of the gas is nitrogen, carbon dioxide, sulphur dioxide, methane, ammonia and hydrogen. The quantity of these gases, again multiplied over 3,500 million years, is enough to explain the mass of the world's atmosphere. We are alive because volcanoes provided the soil, air and water we need.

B Geologists consider the earth as having a molten core, surrounded by a semi-molten mantle and a brittle, outer skin. It helps to think of a soft-boiled egg with a runny yolk, a firm but squishy white and a hard shell. If the shell is even slightly cracked during boiling, the white material bubbles out and sets like a tiny mountain chain over the crack – like an archipelago of volcanic islands such as the Hawaiian Islands. But the earth is so much bigger and the mantle below is so much hotter.

Even though the mantle rocks are kept solid by overlying pressure, they can still slowly 'flow' like thick treacle. The flow, thought to be in the form of convection currents, is powerful enough to fracture the 'eggshell' of the crust into plates, and keep them bumping and grinding against each other, or even overlapping, at the rate of a few centimetres a year. These fracture zones, where the collisions occur, are where earthquakes happen. And, very often, volcanoes.

C These zones are lines of weakness, or hot spots. Every eruption is different, but put at its simplest, where there are weaknesses, rocks deep in the mantle, heated to 1,350°C, will start to expand and rise. As they do so, the pressure drops, and they expand and become liquid and rise more swiftly.

Sometimes it is slow: vast bubbles of magma – molten rock from the mantle – inch towards the surface, cooling slowly, to show through as granite extrusions (as on Skye, or the Great Whin Sill, the lava dyke squeezed out like toothpaste that carries part of Hadrian's Wall in northern England). Sometimes – as in Northern Ireland, Wales and the Karoo in South Africa – the magma rose faster, and then flowed out horizontally on to the surface in vast thick sheets. In the Deccan plateau in western India, there are more than two million cubic kilometres of lava, some of it 2,400 metres thick, formed over 500,000 years of slurping eruption.

Sometimes the magma moves very swiftly indeed. It does not have time to cool as it surges upwards. The gases trapped inside the boiling rock expand suddenly, the lava glows with heat, it begins to froth, and it explodes with tremendous force. Then the slightly cooler lava following it begins to flow over the lip of the crater. It happens on Mars, it happened on the moon, it even happens on some of the moons of Jupiter and Uranus. By studying the evidence, vulcanologists can read the force of the great blasts of the past. Is the pumice light and full of holes? The explosion was tremendous. Are the rocks heavy, with huge crystalline basalt shapes, like the Giant's Causeway in Northern Ireland? It was a slow, gentle eruption.

The biggest eruptions are deep on the mid-ocean floor, where new lava is forcing the continents apart and widening the Atlantic by perhaps five centimetres a year. Look at maps of volcanoes, earthquakes and island chains like the Philippines and Japan, and you can see the rough outlines of what are called tectonic plates – the plates which make up the earth's crust and mantle. The most dramatic of these is the Pacific 'ring of fire' where there have been the most violent explosions – Mount Pinatubo near Manila, Mount St Helen's in the Rockies and El Chichón in Mexico about a decade ago, not to mention world-shaking blasts like Krakatoa in the Sunda Straits in 1883.

D But volcanoes are not very predictable. That is because geological time is not like human time. During quiet periods, volcanoes cap themselves with their own lava by forming a powerful cone from the molten rocks slopping over the rim of the crater; later the lava cools slowly into a huge, hard, stable plug which blocks any further eruption until the pressure below becomes irresistible. In the case of Mount Pinatubo, this took 600 years.

Then, sometimes, with only a small warning, the mountain blows its top. It did this at Mont Pelée in Martinique at 7.49 a.m. on 8 May, 1902. Of a town of 28,000, only two people survived. In 1815, a sudden blast removed the top 1,280 metres of Mount Tambora in Indonesia. The eruption was so fierce that dust thrown into the stratosphere darkened the skies, cancelling the following summer in Europe and North America. Thousands starved as the harvests failed, after snow in June and frosts in August. Volcanoes are potentially world news, especially the quiet ones.

Questions 18–21

Answer the questions below using **NO MORE THAN THREE WORDS AND/OR A NUMBER** *from the passage for each answer.*

Write your answers in boxes 18–21 on your answer sheet.

18   What are the sections of the earth's crust, often associated with volcanic activity, called?

19   What is the name given to molten rock from the mantle?

20   What is the earthquake zone on the Pacific Ocean called?

21   For how many years did Mount Pinatubo remain inactive?

Questions 22–26

Complete the summary below.

Choose **NO MORE THAN TWO WORDS** *from the passage for each answer.*

Write your answers in boxes 22–26 on your answer sheet.

Volcanic eruptions have shaped the earth's land surface. They may also have produced the world's atmosphere and **22**…… . Eruptions occur when molten rocks from the earth's mantle rise and expand. When they become liquid, they move more quickly through cracks in the surface. There are different types of eruption. Sometimes the **23**…… moves slowly and forms outcrops of granite on the earth's surface. When it moves more quickly it may flow out in thick horizontal sheets. Examples of this type of eruption can be found in Northern Ireland, Wales, South Africa and **24**…… . A third type of eruption occurs when the lava emerges very quickly and **25**…… violently. This happens because the magma moves so suddenly that **26**…… are emitted.

READING PASSAGE 3

*You should spend about 20 minutes on **Questions 27–40** which are based on Reading Passage 3 below.*

Obtaining Linguistic Data

A Many procedures are available for obtaining data about a language. They range from a carefully planned, intensive field investigation in a foreign country to a casual introspection about one's mother tongue carried out in an armchair at home.

B In all cases, someone has to act as a source of language data – an *informant*. Informants are (ideally) native speakers of a language, who provide utterances for analysis and other kinds of information about the language (e.g. translations, comments about correctness, or judgements on usage). Often, when studying their mother tongue, linguists act as their own informants, judging the ambiguity, acceptability, or other properties of utterances against their own intuitions. The convenience of this approach makes it widely used, and it is considered the norm in the generative approach to linguistics. But a linguist's personal judgements are often uncertain, or disagree with the judgements of other linguists, at which point recourse is needed to more objective methods of enquiry, using non-linguists as informants.

The latter procedure is unavoidable when working on foreign languages, or child speech.

C Many factors must be considered when selecting informants – whether one is working with single speakers (a common situation when languages have not been described before), two people interacting, small groups or large-scale samples. Age, sex, social background and other aspects of identity are important, as these factors are known to influence the kind of language used. The topic of conversation and the characteristics of the social setting (e.g. the level of formality) are also highly relevant, as are the personal qualities of the informants (e.g. their fluency and consistency). For larger studies, scrupulous attention has been paid to the sampling theory employed, and in all cases, decisions have to be made about the best investigative techniques to use.

D Today, researchers often tape-record informants. This enables the linguist's claims about the language to be checked, and provides a way of making those claims more accurate ('difficult' pieces of speech can be listened to repeatedly). But obtaining naturalistic, good-quality data is never easy. People talk abnormally when they know they are being recorded, and sound quality can be poor. A variety of tape-recording procedures have thus been devised to minimise the 'observer's paradox' (how to observe the way people behave when they are not being observed). Some recordings are made without the speakers being aware of the fact – a procedure that obtains very natural data, though ethical objections must be anticipated. Alternatively, attempts can be made to make the speaker forget about the recording, such as keeping the tape recorder out of sight, or using radio microphones. A useful technique is to introduce a topic that quickly involves the speaker, and stimulates a natural language style (e.g. asking older informants about how times have changed in their locality).

E An audio tape recording does not solve all the linguist's problems, however. Speech is often unclear and ambiguous. Where possible, therefore, the recording has to be supplemented by the observer's written comments on the non-verbal behaviour of the participants, and about the context in general. A facial expression, for example, can dramatically alter the meaning of what is said. Video recordings avoid these problems to a large extent, but even they have limitations (the camera cannot be everywhere), and transcriptions always benefit from any additional commentary provided by an observer.

F Linguists also make great use of structured sessions, in which they systematically ask their informants for utterances that describe certain actions, objects or behaviours. With a bilingual informant, or through use of an inter-

preter, it is possible to use translation techniques ('How do you say *table* in your language?'). A large number of points can be covered in a short time, using interview worksheets and questionnaires. Often, the researcher wishes to obtain information about just a single variable, in which case a restricted set of questions may be used: a particular feature of pronunciation, for example, can be elicited by asking the informant to say a restricted set of words. There are also several direct methods of elicitation, such as asking informants to fill in the blanks in a substitution frame (e.g. *I ___ see a car*), or feeding them the wrong stimulus for correction ('Is it possible to say *I no can see*?').

G A representative sample of language, compiled for the purpose of linguistic analysis, is known as a *corpus*. A corpus enables the linguist to make unbiased statements about frequency of usage, and it provides accessible data for the use of different researchers. Its range and size are variable. Some corpora attempt to cover the language as a whole, taking extracts from many kinds of text; others are extremely selective, providing a collection of material that deals only with a particular linguistic feature. The size of the corpus depends on practical factors, such as the time available to collect, process and store the data: it can take up to several hours to provide an accurate transcription of a few minutes of speech. Sometimes a small sample of data will be enough to decide a linguistic hypothesis; by contrast, corpora in major research projects can total millions of words. An important principle is that all corpora, whatever their size, are inevitably limited in their coverage, and always need to be supplemented by data derived from the intuitions of native speakers of the language, through either introspection or experimentation.

Questions 27–31

Reading Passage 3 has seven paragraphs labelled **A–G**.

Which paragraph contains the following information?

*Write the correct letter **A–G** in boxes 27–31 on your answer sheet.*

NB *You may use any letter more than once.*

27 the effect of recording on the way people talk

28 the importance of taking notes on body language

29 the fact that language is influenced by social situation

30 how informants can be helped to be less self-conscious

31 various methods that can be used to generate specific data

Questions 32–36

Complete the table below.

*Choose **NO MORE THAN THREE WORDS** from the passage for each answer.*

Write your answers in boxes 32–36 on your answer sheet.

METHODS OF OBTAINING LINGUISTIC DATA	ADVANTAGES	DISADVANTAGES
32...... as informant	convenient	method of enquiry not objective enough
non-linguist as informant	necessary with **33**...... and child speech	the number of factors to be considered
recording an informant	allows linguists' claims to be checked	**34**...... of sound
videoing an informant	allows speakers' **35**...... to be observed	**36**...... might miss certain things

Questions 37–40

Complete the summary of paragraph G below.

*Choose **NO MORE THAN THREE WORDS** from the passage for each answer.*

Write your answers in boxes 37–40 on your answer sheet.

A linguist can use a corpus to comment objectively on **37**...... . Some corpora include a wide range of language while others are used to focus on a **38**...... . The length of time the process takes will affect the **39**...... of the corpus. No corpus can ever cover the whole language and so linguists often find themselves relying on the additional information that can be gained from the **40**...... of those who speak the language concerned.

WRITING

WRITING TASK 1

You should spend about 20 minutes on this task.

> *The chart below shows the different levels of post-school qualifications in Australia and the proportion of men and women who held them in 1999.*
>
> *Summarise the information by selecting and reporting the main features, and make comparisons where relevant.*

Write at least 150 words.

Post-school qualifications in Australia according to gender 1999

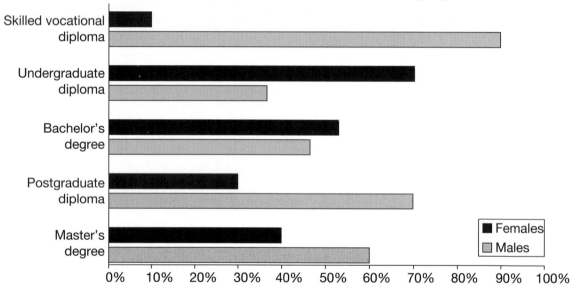

WRITING TASK 2

You should spend about 40 minutes on this task.

Write about the following topic:

> *Creative artists should always be given the freedom to express their own ideas (in words, pictures, music or film) in whichever way they wish. There should be no government restrictions on what they do.*
>
> *To what extent do you agree or disagree with this opinion?*

Give reasons for your answer and include any relevant examples from your own knowledge or experience.

Write at least 250 words.

SPEAKING

PART 1

The examiner asks the candidate about him/herself, his/her home, work or studies and other familiar topics.

EXAMPLE

Leisure

- Do you have any hobbies or interests? [What are they?]
- How did you become interested in (*whatever hobby/interest the candidate mentions*)?
- What is there to do in your free time in (*candidate's home town/village*)?
- How do you usually spend your holidays?
- Is there anywhere you would particularly like to visit? [Why?]

PART 2

Describe a river, lake or sea which you like. **You should say:** 　　**what the river, lake or sea is called** 　　**where it is** 　　**what the land near it is like** **and explain why you like this river, lake or sea.**

You will have to talk about the topic for one to two minutes.
You have one minute to think about what you're going to say.
You can make some notes to help you if you wish.

PART 3

Discussion topics:

Water-based leisure activities

Example questions:
What do people enjoy doing when they visit rivers, lakes or the sea? Why do you think these activities are popular?
What benefits do you think people get from the activities they enjoy in the water?
What are the different advantages of going to the sea or to a swimming pool to enjoy yourself? What do you think the disadvantages are?

The economic importance of rivers, lakes and the sea

Example questions:
How does water transport, like boats and ships, compare with other kinds? Are there any advantages/disadvantages of water transport?
How important is it for a town or city to be located near a river or the sea? Why?
Have there been any changes in the number of jobs available in fishing and water transport industries, do you think? Why do you think this is?

Test 4

LISTENING

SECTION 1   *Questions 1–10*

Questions 1–10

Complete the notes below.

*Write **NO MORE THAN THREE WORDS AND/OR A NUMBER** for each answer.*

GOODBYE PARTY FOR JOHN

Example	*Answer*
Date:	*22nd December*

Venue: **1** ....

Invitations (Tony)

Who to invite:
– John and his wife
– Director
– the **2** ....
– all the teachers
– all the **3** ....

Date for sending invitations: **4** ....

Present (Lisa)

Collect money during the   **5** ....

Suggested amount per person: **6** $ ....

Check prices for:
– CD players
– **7** ....
– coffee maker

Ask guests to bring:
– snacks
– **8** ....
– **9** ....

Ask student representative to prepare a   **10** ....

SECTION 2 *Questions 11–20*

Questions 11–15

*Choose the correct letter, **A**, **B** or **C**.*

11 To find out how much holidays cost, you should press button

    A   one.
    B   two.
    C   three.

12 Travelite currently offer walking holidays

    A   only in Western Europe.
    B   all over Europe.
    C   outside Europe.

13 The walks offered by Travelite

    A   cater for a range of walking abilities.
    B   are planned by guides from the local area.
    C   are for people with good fitness levels.

14 On Travelite holidays, people holidaying alone pay

    A   the same as other clients.
    B   only a little more than other clients.
    C   extra only if they stay in a large room.

15 Entertainment is provided

    A   when guests request it.
    B   most nights.
    C   every night.

Questions 16–20

Complete the table below.

Write **NO MORE THAN THREE WORDS AND/OR A NUMBER** *for each answer.*

Length of holiday	Cost per person (including all accommodation costs)	Special offers included in price
3 days	**16** $........................	Pick up from the **17** ....
7 days	$350	As above plus • book of **18** .... • maps
14 days	**19** $........................	As above plus membership of a **20** ....

SECTION 3   *Questions 21–30*

Questions 21–26

Complete the table below.

*Write **NO MORE THAN THREE WORDS AND/OR A NUMBER** for each answer.*

Experiment number	Equipment	Purpose
Experiment 1	**21** .... and a table	To show how things move on a cushion of air
Experiment 2	Lots of paperclips	To show why we need standard **22** ....
Experiment 3	**23** .... and a jar of water	To show how **24** .... grow
Experiment 4	Cardboard, coloured pens and a **25**	To teach children about how **26** .... is made up
Experiment 5	A drill, an old record, a pin/needle, paper, a bolt	To make a record player in order to learn about recording sound

Questions 27–30

What problems do the speakers identify for each experiment?

*Choose your answers from the box and write the letters **A–H** next to questions 27–30.*

Problems
A too messy
B too boring
C too difficult
D too much equipment
E too long
F too easy ✔
G too noisy
H too dangerous

Experiment 1:   **27** ....

Experiment 2:   **28** ....

Experiment 3:   **29** ....

Experiment 4:   Example **F**

Experiment 5:   **30** ....

SECTION 4   *Questions 31–40*

Questions 31–34

Complete the notes below.

*Write **NO MORE THAN THREE WORDS AND/OR A NUMBER** for each answer.*

Sharks in Australia		
Length	largest caught:	16 metres
Weight	heaviest:	31 .... kg
Skeleton	cartilage	
Skin texture	rough barbs	
Swimming aids	fins and 32	
Food	gathered from the ocean 33	
	sharks locate food by using their 34	

Questions 35–38

*Choose the correct letter, **A**, **B** or **C**.*

35 Shark meshing uses nets laid

    A   along the coastline.
    B   at an angle to the beach.
    C   from the beach to the sea.

36 Other places that have taken up shark meshing include

    A   South Africa.
    B   New Zealand.
    C   Tahiti.

37 The average number of sharks caught in nets each year is

    A   15.
    B   150.
    C   1,500.

38 Most sharks are caught in

    A   spring.
    B   summer.
    C   winter.

Questions 39 and 40

*Choose **TWO** letters A–G.*

*Which **TWO** factors reduce the benefits of shark nets?*

    A   nets wrongly positioned
    B   strong waves and currents
    C   too many fish
    D   sharks eat holes in nets
    E   moving sands
    F   nets too short
    G   holes in nets scare sharks

READING

READING PASSAGE 1

*You should spend about 20 minutes on **Questions 1–13** which are based on Reading Passage 1 below.*

How much higher? How much faster?

— Limits to human sporting performance are not yet in sight —

Since the early years of the twentieth century, when the International Athletic Federation began keeping records, there has been a steady improvement in how fast athletes run, how high they jump and how far they are able to hurl massive objects, themselves included, through space. For the so-called power events – that require a relatively brief, explosive release of energy, like the 100-metre sprint and the long jump – times and distances have improved ten to twenty per cent. In the endurance events the results have been more dramatic. At the 1908 Olympics, John Hayes of the U.S. team ran a marathon in a time of 2:55:18. In 1999, Morocco's Khalid Khannouchi set a new world record of 2:05:42, almost thirty per cent faster.

No one theory can explain improvements in performance, but the most important factor has been genetics. 'The athlete must choose his parents carefully,' says Jesus Dapena, a sports scientist at Indiana University, invoking an oft-cited adage. Over the past century, the composition of the human gene pool has not changed appreciably, but with increasing global participation in athletics – and greater rewards to tempt athletes – it is more likely that individuals possessing the unique complement of genes for athletic performance can be identified early. 'Was there someone like [sprinter] Michael Johnson in the 1920s?' Dapena asks. 'I'm sure there was, but his talent was probably never realised.'

Identifying genetically talented individuals is only the first step. Michael Yessis, an emeritus professor of Sports Science at California State University at Fullerton, maintains that 'genetics only determines about one third of what an athlete can do. But with the right training we can go much further with that one third than we've been going.' Yessis believes that U.S. runners, despite their impressive achievements, are 'running on their genetics'. By applying more scientific methods, 'they're going to go much faster'. These methods include strength training that duplicates what they are doing in their running events as well as plyometrics, a technique pioneered in the former Soviet Union.

Whereas most exercises are designed to build up strength or endurance, plyometrics focuses on increasing power – the rate at which an athlete can expend energy. When a sprinter runs, Yessis explains, her foot stays in contact with the ground for just under a tenth of a second, half of which is devoted to landing and the other half to pushing off. Plyometric exercises help athletes make the best use of this brief interval.

Nutrition is another area that sports trainers have failed to address adequately. 'Many athletes are not getting the best nutrition, even through supplements,' Yessis insists. Each activity has its own nutritional needs. Few coaches, for instance, understand how deficiencies in trace minerals can lead to injuries.

Focused training will also play a role in enabling records to be broken. 'If we applied the Russian training model to some of the outstanding runners we have in this country,' Yessis asserts, 'they would be breaking records left and right.' He will not predict by how much, however: 'Exactly what the limits are it's hard to say, but there will be increases even if only by hundredths of a second, as long as our training continues to improve.'

One of the most important new methodologies is biomechanics, the study of the body in motion. A biomechanic films an athlete in action and then digitizes her performance, recording the motion of every joint and limb in three dimensions. By applying Newton's laws to these motions, 'we can say that this athlete's run is not fast enough; that this one is not using his arms strongly enough during take-off,' says Dapena, who uses these methods to help high jumpers. To date, however, biomechanics has made only a small difference to athletic performance.

Revolutionary ideas still come from the athletes themselves. For example, during the 1968 Olympics in Mexico City, a relatively unknown high jumper named Dick Fosbury won the gold by going over the bar backwards, in complete contradiction of all the received high-jumping wisdom, a move instantly dubbed the Fosbury flop. Fosbury himself did not know what he was doing. That understanding took the later analysis of biomechanics specialists, who put their minds to comprehending something that was too complex and unorthodox ever to have been invented through their own mathematical simulations. Fosbury also required another element that lies behind many improvements in athletic performance: an innovation in athletic equipment. In Fosbury's case, it was the cushions that jumpers land on. Traditionally, high jumpers would land in pits filled with sawdust. But by Fosbury's time, sawdust pits had been replaced by soft foam cushions, ideal for flopping.

In the end, most people who examine human performance are humbled by the resourcefulness of athletes and the powers of the human body. 'Once you study athletics, you learn that it's a vexingly complex issue,' says John S. Raglin, a sports psychologist at Indiana University. 'Core performance is not a simple or mundane thing of higher, faster, longer. So many variables enter into the equation, and our understanding in many cases is fundamental. We've got a long way to go.' For the foreseeable future, records will be made to be broken.

Questions 1–6

Do the following statements agree with the information given in Reading Passage 1?

In boxes 1–6 on your answer sheet write

> **TRUE**   *if the statement agrees with the information*
> **FALSE**   *if the statement contradicts the information*
> **NOT GIVEN** *if there is no information on this*

1   Modern official athletic records date from about 1900.

2   There was little improvement in athletic performance before the twentieth century.

3   Performance has improved most greatly in events requiring an intensive burst of energy.

4   Improvements in athletic performance can be fully explained by genetics.

5   The parents of top athletes have often been successful athletes themselves.

6   The growing international importance of athletics means that gifted athletes can be recognised at a younger age.

Questions 7–10

Complete the sentences below with words taken from Reading Passage 1.

*Use **ONE WORD** for each answer.*

Write your answers in boxes 7–10 on your answer sheet.

7   According to Professor Yessis, American runners are relying for their current success on ....

8   Yessis describes a training approach from the former Soviet Union that aims to develop an athlete's ....

9   Yessis links an inadequate diet to ....

10   Yessis claims that the key to setting new records is better ....

Questions 11–13

*Choose the correct letter, **A**, **B**, **C** or **D**.*

Write your answers in boxes 11–13 on your answer sheet.

11 Biomechanics films are proving particularly useful because they enable trainers to

    A   highlight areas for improvement in athletes.
    B   assess the fitness levels of athletes.
    C   select top athletes.
    D   predict the success of athletes.

12 Biomechanics specialists used theoretical models to

    A   soften the Fosbury flop.
    B   create the Fosbury flop.
    C   correct the Fosbury flop.
    D   explain the Fosbury flop.

13 John S. Raglin believes our current knowledge of athletics is

    A   mistaken.
    B   basic.
    C   diverse.
    D   theoretical.

READING PASSAGE 2

*You should spend about 20 minutes on **Questions 14–27** which are based on Reading Passage 2 below.*

THE NATURE AND AIMS OF ARCHAEOLOGY

Archaeology is partly the discovery of the treasures of the past, partly the careful work of the scientific analyst, partly the exercise of the creative imagination. It is toiling in the sun on an excavation in the Middle East, it is working with living Inuit in the snows of Alaska, and it is investigating the sewers of Roman Britain. But it is also the painstaking task of interpretation, so that we come to understand what these things mean for the human story. And it is the conservation of the world's cultural heritage against looting and careless harm.

Archaeology, then, is both a physical activity out in the field, and an intellectual pursuit in the study or laboratory. That is part of its great attraction. The rich mixture of danger and detective work has also made it the perfect vehicle for fiction writers and film-makers, from Agatha Christie with *Murder in Mesopotamia* to Stephen Spielberg with *Indiana Jones*. However far from reality such portrayals are, they capture the essential truth that archaeology is an exciting quest – the quest for knowledge about ourselves and our past.

But how does archaeology relate to disciplines such as anthropology and history, that are also concerned with the human story? Is archaeology itself a science? And what are the responsibilities of the archaeologist in today's world?

Anthropology, at its broadest, is the study of humanity – our physical characteristics as animals and our unique non-biological characteristics that we call culture. Culture in this sense includes what the anthropologist, Edward Tylor, summarised in 1871 as 'knowledge, belief, art, morals, custom and any other capabilities and habits acquired by man as a member of society'. Anthropologists also use the term 'culture' in a more restricted sense when they refer to the 'culture' of a particular society, meaning the non-biological characteristics unique to that society, which distinguish it from other societies. Anthropology is thus a broad discipline – so broad that it is generally broken down into three smaller disciplines: physical anthropology, cultural anthropology and archaeology.

Physical anthropology, or biological anthropology as it is also called, concerns the study of human biological or physical characteristics and how they evolved. Cultural anthropology – or social anthropology – analyses human culture and society. Two of its branches are ethnography (the study at first hand of individual living cultures) and ethnology (which sets out to compare cultures using ethnographic evidence to derive general principles about human society).

Archaeology is the 'past tense of cultural anthropology'. Whereas cultural anthropologists will often base their conclusions on the experience of living within contemporary communities, archaeologists study past societies primarily through their material remains – the buildings, tools, and other artefacts that constitute what is known as the material culture left over from former societies.

Nevertheless, one of the most important tasks for the archaeologist today is to know how to interpret material culture in human terms. How were those pots used? Why are some dwellings round and others square? Here the methods of archaeology and ethnography overlap. Archaeologists in recent decades have developed 'ethnoarchaeology', where, like ethnographers, they live among contemporary communities, but with the specific purpose of learning how such societies use material culture – how they make their tools and weapons, why they build their settlements where they do, and so on. Moreover, archaeology has an active role to play in the field of conservation. Heritage studies constitutes a developing field, where it is realised that the world's cultural heritage is a diminishing resource which holds different meanings for different people.

If, then, archaeology deals with the past, in what way does it differ from history? In the broadest sense, just as archaeology is an aspect of anthropology, so too is it a part of history – where we mean the whole history of humankind from its beginnings over three million years ago. Indeed, for more than ninety-nine per cent of that huge span of time, archaeology – the study of past material culture – is the only significant source of information. Conventional historical sources begin only with the introduction of written records around 3,000 BC in western Asia, and much later in most other parts of the world.

A commonly drawn distinction is between pre-history, i.e. the period before written records – and history in the narrow sense, meaning the study of the past using written evidence. To archaeology, which studies all cultures and periods, whether with or without writing, the distinction between history and pre-history is a convenient dividing line that recognises the importance of the written word, but in no way lessens the importance of the useful information contained in oral histories.

Since the aim of archaeology is the understanding of humankind, it is a humanistic study, and since it deals with the human past, it is a historical discipline. But it differs from the study of written history in a fundamental way. The material the archaeologist finds does not tell us directly what to think. Historical records make statements, offer opinions and pass judgements. The objects the archaeologists discover, on the other hand, tell us nothing directly in themselves. In this respect, the practice of the archaeologist is rather like that of the scientist, who collects data, conducts experiments, formulates a hypothesis, tests the hypothesis against more data, and then, in conclusion, devises a model that seems best to summarise the pattern observed in the data. The archaeologist has to develop a picture of the past, just as the scientist has to develop a coherent view of the natural world.

Questions 14–19

Do the following statements agree with the claims of the writer in Reading Passage 2?

In boxes 14–19 on your answer sheet write

>**YES** if the statement agrees with the claims of the writer
>**NO** if the statement contradicts the claims of the writer
>**NOT GIVEN** *if it is impossible to say what the writer thinks about this*

14 Archaeology involves creativity as well as careful investigative work.

15 Archaeologists must be able to translate texts from ancient languages.

16 Movies give a realistic picture of the work of archaeologists.

17 Anthropologists define culture in more than one way.

18 Archaeology is a more demanding field of study than anthropology.

19 The history of Europe has been documented since 3,000 BC.

Questions 20 and 21

*Choose **TWO** letters A–E.*

Write your answers in boxes 20 and 21 on your answer sheet.

The list below gives some statements about anthropology.

Which **TWO** statements are mentioned by the writer of the text?

>**A** It is important for government planners.
>**B** It is a continually growing field of study.
>**C** It often involves long periods of fieldwork.
>**D** It is subdivided for study purposes.
>**E** It studies human evolutionary patterns.

Questions 22 and 23

*Choose **TWO** letters A–E.*

Write your answers in boxes 22 and 23 on your answer sheet.

The list below gives some of the tasks of an archaeologist.

Which **TWO** of these tasks are mentioned by the writer of the text?

    A   examining ancient waste sites to investigate diet
    B   studying cave art to determine its significance
    C   deducing reasons for the shape of domestic buildings
    D   investigating the way different cultures make and use objects
    E   examining evidence for past climate changes

Questions 24–27

Complete the summary of the last two paragraphs of Reading Passage 2.

*Choose **NO MORE THAN TWO WORDS** from the passage for each answer.*

Write your answers in boxes 24–27 on your answer sheet.

Much of the work of archaeologists can be done using written records but they find **24**…… equally valuable. The writer describes archaeology as both a **25**…… and a **26**…… . However, as archaeologists do not try to influence human behaviour, the writer compares their style of working to that of a **27**…… .

READING PASSAGE 3

*You should spend about 20 minutes on **Questions 28–40** which are based on Reading Passage 3 on the following pages.*

Questions 28–31

Reading Passage 3 has five sections **A–E**.

*Choose the correct heading for sections **A** and **C–E** from the list of headings below.*

*Write the correct number **i–viii** in boxes 28–31 on your answer sheet.*

List of Headings
i   The connection between health-care and other human rights
ii   The development of market-based health systems
iii   The role of the state in health-care
iv   A problem shared by every economically developed country
v   The impact of recent change
vi   The views of the medical establishment
vii   The end of an illusion
viii   Sustainable economic development

28   Section **A**

Example	*Answer*
Section **B**	**viii**

29   Section **C**

30   Section **D**

31   Section **E**

The Problem of Scarce Resources

Section A

The problem of how health-care resources should be allocated or apportioned, so that they are distributed in both the most just and most efficient way, is not a new one. Every health system in an economically developed society is faced with the need to decide (either formally or informally) what proportion of the community's total resources should be spent on health-care; how resources are to be apportioned; what diseases and disabilities and which forms of treatment are to be given priority; which members of the community are to be given special consideration in respect of their health needs; and which forms of treatment are the most cost-effective.

Section B

What is new is that, from the 1950s onwards, there have been certain general changes in outlook about the finitude of resources as a whole and of health-care resources in particular, as well as more specific changes regarding the clientele of health-care resources and the cost to the community of those resources. Thus, in the 1950s and 1960s, there emerged an awareness in Western societies that resources for the provision of fossil fuel energy were finite and exhaustible and that the capacity of nature or the environment to sustain economic development and population was also finite. In other words, we became aware of the obvious fact that there were 'limits to growth'. The new consciousness that there were also severe limits to health-care resources was part of this general revelation of the obvious. Looking back, it now seems quite incredible that in the national health systems that emerged in many countries in the years immediately after the 1939–45 World War, it was assumed without question that all the basic health needs of any community could be satisfied, at least in principle; the 'invisible hand' of economic progress would provide.

Section C

However, at exactly the same time as this new realisation of the finite character of health-care resources was sinking in, an awareness of a contrary kind was developing in Western societies: that people have a basic right to health-care as a necessary condition of a proper human life. Like education, political and legal processes and institutions, public order, communication, transport and money supply, health-care came to be seen as one of the fundamental social facilities necessary for people to exercise their other rights as autonomous human beings. People are not in a position to exercise personal liberty and to be self-determining if they are poverty-stricken, or deprived of basic education, or do not live within a context of law and order. In the same way, basic health-care is a condition of the exercise of autonomy.

Section D

Although the language of 'rights' sometimes leads to confusion, by the late 1970s it was recognised in most societies that people have a right to health-care (though there has been considerable resistance in the United States to the idea that there is a formal right to health-care). It is also accepted that this right generates an obligation or duty for the state to ensure that adequate health-care resources are provided out of the public purse. The state has no obligation to provide a health-care system itself, but to ensure that such a system is provided. Put another way, basic health-care is now recognised as a 'public good', rather than a 'private good' that one is expected to buy for oneself. As the 1976 declaration of the World Health Organisation put it: 'The enjoyment of the highest attainable standard of health is one of the fundamental rights of every human being without distinction of race, religion, political belief, economic or social condition.' As has just been remarked, in a liberal society basic health is seen as one of the indispensable conditions for the exercise of personal autonomy.

Section E

Just at the time when it became obvious that health-care resources could not possibly meet the demands being made upon them, people were demanding that their fundamental right to health-care be satisfied by the state. The second set of more specific changes that have led to the present concern about the distribution of health-care resources stems from the dramatic rise in health costs in most OECD[1] countries, accompanied by large-scale demographic and social changes which have meant, to take one example, that elderly people are now major (and relatively very expensive) consumers of health-care resources. Thus in OECD countries as a whole, health costs increased from 3.8% of GDP[2] in 1960 to 7% of GDP in 1980, and it has been predicted that the proportion of health costs to GDP will continue to increase. (In the US the current figure is about 12% of GDP, and in Australia about 7.8% of GDP.)

As a consequence, during the 1980s a kind of doomsday scenario (analogous to similar doomsday extrapolations about energy needs and fossil fuels or about population increases) was projected by health administrators, economists and politicians. In this scenario, ever-rising health costs were matched against static or declining resources.

---

1 Organisation for Economic Cooperation and Development

2 Gross Domestic Product

Questions 32–35

Classify the following as first occurring

    A *between 1945 and 1950*
    B *between 1950 and 1980*
    C *after 1980*

*Write the correct letter **A**, **B** or **C** in boxes 32–35 on your answer sheet.*

32   the realisation that the resources of the national health systems were limited

33   a sharp rise in the cost of health-care

34   a belief that all the health-care resources the community needed would be produced by economic growth

35   an acceptance of the role of the state in guaranteeing the provision of health-care

Questions 36–40

Do the following statements agree with the views of the writer in Reading Passage 3?

In boxes 36–40 on your answer sheet write

    YES   *if the statement agrees with the views of the writer*
    NO   *if the statement contradicts the views of the writer*
    NOT GIVEN *if it is impossible to say what the writer thinks about this*

36   Personal liberty and independence have never been regarded as directly linked to health-care.

37   Health-care came to be seen as a right at about the same time that the limits of health-care resources became evident.

38   In OECD countries population changes have had an impact on health-care costs in recent years.

39   OECD governments have consistently underestimated the level of health-care provision needed.

40   In most economically developed countries the elderly will have to make special provision for their health-care in the future.

WRITING

WRITING TASK 1

You should spend about 20 minutes on this task.

> *The charts below give information about travel to and from the UK, and about the most popular countries for UK residents to visit.*
>
> *Summarise the information by selecting and reporting the main features, and make comparisons where relevant.*

Write at least 150 words.

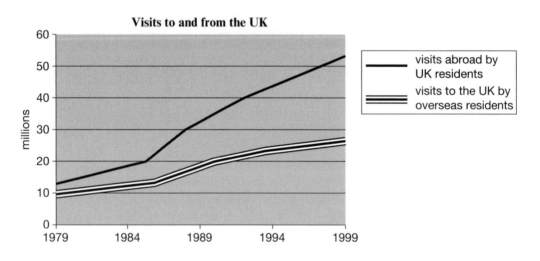

Visits to and from the UK

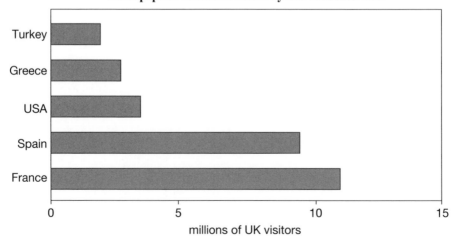

Most popular countries visited by UK residents 1999

WRITING TASK 2

You should spend about 40 minutes on this task.

Write about the following topic:

> *In many countries schools have severe problems with student behaviour.*
>
> *What do you think are the causes of this?*
>
> *What solutions can you suggest?*

Give reasons for your answer and include any relevant examples from your own knowledge or experience.

Write at least 250 words.

SPEAKING

PART 1

The examiner asks the candidate about him/herself, his/her home, work or studies and other familiar topics.

EXAMPLE

Your favourite place

- What place do you most like to visit?
- How often do you visit this place?
- Why do you like it so much?
- Is it popular with many other people?
- Has it changed very much since you first went there? [In what way?]

PART 2

Describe a useful website you have visited.
You should say:
   what the website was
   how you found the address for this website
   what the website contained
and explain why it was useful to you.

You will have to talk about the topic for one to two minutes.
You have one minute to think about what you're going to say.
You can make some notes to help you if you wish.

PART 3

Discussion topics:

The internet and communication

Example questions:
What effect has the internet had on the way people generally communicate with each other?
Why do you think the internet is being used more and more for communication?
How reliable do you think information from the internet is? Why? What about the news on the internet?

The internet and shopping

Example questions:
Why do you think some people use the internet for shopping? Why doesn't everyone use it in this way?
What kinds of things are easy to buy and sell online? Can you give me some examples?
Do you think shopping on the internet will be more or less popular in the future? Why?

General Training: Reading and Writing Test A

READING

SECTION 1   *Questions 1–14*

Questions 1–5

Look at the five restaurant advertisements A–E below.

For which restaurant are the following statements true?

Write the correct letter A–E in boxes 1–5 on your answer sheet.

NB You may use any letter more than once.

1   You can't eat at this restaurant on Monday evening.

2   You can have a meal here in peaceful country surroundings.

3   You can eat here on a Sunday night.

4   You can have your order delivered for an extra fee.

5   You can have dinner here and then stay the night.

A

THE AUTHENTIC TASTE OF THAILAND

CHANGTOM

THAI RESTAURANT AND HOTEL

12–3 6–12 CLOSED SUNDAYS

- SET IN 40 ACRES OF SCENIC WOODLAND
- OUTSIDE DINING AREA
- FRESH PRODUCE ALWAYS USED
- CREDIT CARDS ACCEPTED
- SEATING FOR UP TO 50
- FULLY LICENSED BAR
- SMALL FUNCTION ROOM AVAILABLE FOR HIRE
- LUXURY ACCOMMODATION AVAILABLE
- EASY PARKING
- VIEWS OVER BEAUTIFUL LANDSCAPED GARDENS

FOR THE FINEST STANDARDS OF CUISINE & SERVICE

B

JACK'S

TRADITIONAL AND AMERICAN RESTAURANT

For a Family Treat or that Special Occasion…

- SUPERB SELECTION OF CLASSIC AMERICAN BURGERS & STEAKS
- FISH & CHIPS & VEGETARIAN PLUS CHILDREN'S MENU
- LICENSED BAR
- WEDDINGS & PARTY BOOKINGS WELCOME
- TAKEAWAY SERVICE

**LUNCHTIMES
TUESDAY – SATURDAY
EVENINGS
WEDNESDAY – SATURDAY**

103

C

MOGHUL EXPRESS
INDIAN TAKEAWAY

ENJOY FINE INDIAN FOOD IN THE COMFORT OF YOUR HOME
OPEN 7 DAYS A WEEK INCLUDING PUBLIC HOLIDAYS
GOOD PARKING FACILITIES
HOME DELIVERY SERVICE WITHIN A 4-MILE RADIUS OF
OUR TAKEAWAY – SMALL CHARGE

TEL: NORWICH 420988/588980

TOP UK TAKEAWAY AWARD & HYGIENE & QUALITY AWARD
FOR TWO YEARS RUNNING

D

THE MARINA RESTAURANT

OPEN ALL DAY FOR
DELICIOUS INTERNATIONAL CUISINE AT LOCAL PRICES
WE HAVE A CONSTANTLY CHANGING MENU OF HOME-PRODUCED FRESH FOOD
USING ONLY THE BEST LOCAL PRODUCE
* BUSINESS LUNCHES * ANNIVERSARIES AND WEDDINGS * ALL SPECIAL OCCASIONS
SNACKS & LIGHT MEALS, LUNCHES & DINNERS, FULL BAR & EXTENSIVE WINE LIST
DINE IN STYLE ABOARD THE MARINA IN RELAXED & INFORMAL SURROUNDINGS &
SAMPLE THE PLEASURES OF NORWICH'S PREMIER RESTAURANT
OPEN ALL DAY, MON–SAT
LARGE VIDEO SCANNED CAR PARK OPPOSITE

E

PEKING HOUSE

RESTAURANT AND TAKEAWAY

DELICIOUS HIGH CLASS
CHINESE FOOD COOKED BY
EXPERIENCED CHEFS IN OUR
OWN UNIQUE & ULTRA-MODERN
KITCHENS

FREE DELIVERY – AMPLE CAR
PARK

TELEPHONE ORDERS WELCOME

ASK ABOUT OUR CHEF'S
SPECIALITY

	LUNCHTIME	EVENING
SUNDAY	CLOSED	5–11 pm
MONDAY	CLOSED	5–11.30 pm
TUESDAY	CLOSED	5–11.30 pm
WEDNESDAY	CLOSED	5–11.30 pm
THURSDAY	CLOSED	5–11.30 pm
FRIDAY	CLOSED	5–midnight
SATURDAY	CLOSED	5–midnight

NORWICH (01603) 571122
40 QUEEN STREET, NORWICH

Read the extracts below and answer Questions 6–14.

A   RICHMOND EXPERIMENTAL THEATRE

Learn to act introduces people to a broad range of acting techniques. It is specially geared to those with little or no acting experience. The atmosphere is relaxed and unthreatening and great emphasis is placed on developing the confidence and abilities of people who may initially be a little apprehensive!

B   WORLD CULTURE DAY

Brazilian Street Percussion
2.30–4.30
Samba percussion workshop. Lift your spirits with the taste of carnival! It doesn't matter whether you're an experienced musician or a complete beginner, you'll be creating complex exotic rhythms in no time.

African Storytelling
3.45–4.45
The magical African story-telling tradition of narration, poetry and proverbs (mainly from Ghana and Nigeria). An event for all the family.

C   SCOTTISH DANCING

IT'S FUN
IT'S GOOD EXERCISE
- We have classes for dancers of all abilities.
- Previous experience is not essential.
- All you need to bring is a pair of soft shoes and enthusiasm.
- Classes are held in a number of places and at different times.
- We guarantee you a warm welcome.

D   THE RENAISSANCE SINGERS

New singers are invited to join our choir, formed in 1993, to perform a wide variety of music in Cambridge. We meet every Wednesday evening from 7.30–9.30 pm, and this term we are rehearsing for a special concert with audience participation on Saturday 1st December.
An ability to sight-read and previous experience in choral singing is desirable, although not essential.

E   DRAWING WITH COLOUR

An intensive workshop for beginners
Saturday 13th and Sunday 14th October
This unusual workshop offers instruction in effective ways to draw in colour. Activities will include study of light and shade and ways to express mood and emotion in colour.
The small class (12 students) assures maximum attention for each student. Professional quality materials are included in the fee of £95.

Questions 6–14

The passage on the previous page has five sections **A–E**.

For which section are the following statements true?

*Write the correct letter **A–E** in boxes 6–14 on your answer sheet.*

NB *You may use any letter more than once.*

6   A friendly greeting awaits new members.

7   Some relevant skills are preferred.

8   This activity could cheer you up.

9   This activity is suitable for a variety of ages.

10   Individual guidance will be provided.

11   Participants can take part in a public performance.

12   This activity could help someone who wants to overcome shyness.

13   This activity promises rapid progress.

14   This activity is not held during the day.

SECTION 2   *Questions 15–27*

Read the passage below and answer Questions 15–20.

STUDENT LIFE AT CANTERBURY COLLEGE

Most of the courses at Canterbury College only take up four days of the week, leaving one day free for independent study.

The atmosphere at the College is that of an adult environment where a relationship of mutual respect is encouraged between students and tutors.

Canterbury is a student city with several institutes of Further and Higher Education. The city centre is just a five-minute walk from the College, easily accessible in lunch or study breaks.

Canterbury College has developed strong international links over the years and, as a result, many students have the opportunity of visiting and working in a European country in the course of their studies.

Students' Union and SRC
All students are automatically members of the Canterbury College Students' Union (CCSU) and can attend meetings. The Union is very active and is run by an Executive Committee elected by students in the Autumn Term. The President is elected every Summer Term to provide continuity for the next academic year. Representatives from each area of study form the Student Representative Council (SRC) which allows every student a say in Union affairs. In addition to representing students internally in the College on the Academic Board and with a sub-committee of the College Corporation, the CCSU also belongs to the National Union of Students which represents the interests of students nationally. The Union also arranges and supports entertainments, sporting activities and trips.

STUDENT FACILITIES
Learning Resources Centre (LRC)
The Carey Learning Resources Centre provides easy access to a wide range of printed and audio-visual learning materials which can help students with coursework. There is ample space for quiet independent study and there are also areas for group work. Resources provided include books, journals, audio and video cassettes and CD-ROMs. Inter-library loans are available locally and nationally via the British Library. All students are encouraged to use the Open Access Information Technology Centre situated on the first floor. This has a variety of computing, word processing and desktop publishing software.

Bookshop
A branch of Waterstone's bookshops is located on campus, where you can buy a range of stationery, drawing equipment, artists' materials and books, as well as many other useful items you may need.

Children's Centre
The College Children's Centre has places for under 5s with some subsidised places being available to students. Places are limited, so, if you are interested, apply early to reserve a place by contacting Linda Baker on the College telephone number.

Refectory
This provides refreshments between 08.30 and 19.00 with hot meals served three times a day. Healthy eating options are available.

Coffee Shop
This is open during normal College hours and serves light snacks and drinks. Proceeds from the Coffee Shop go to the Students' Union.

Crypt Restaurant
This is a training restaurant which offers good quality cuisine in pleasant surroundings. Meals are very reasonably priced and you are invited to sample the students' highly skilled dishes when the restaurant is open to the public during the week. Reservations can be made on 01227 511244.

Chapel View Restaurant
This is another training restaurant and is set up as a quick-service facility which offers a selection of snacks and main courses at a modest price.

Questions 15–20

Read the passage on the previous page about student life at Canterbury College.

Do the following statements agree with the information given in the passage?

In boxes 15–20 on your answer sheet write

> **TRUE** *if the statement agrees with the information*
> **FALSE** *if the statement contradicts the information*
> **NOT GIVEN** *if there is no information on this*

15 Many students are allocated a job experience placement abroad.

16 The elections for the Union President and Executive Committee are held together.

17 There are staff in the LRC to help students use the facilities.

18 Nursery care is available on a first-come, first-served basis.

19 The Refectory serves fast-food options.

20 The Chapel View Restaurant is for students only.

Read the passage below and answer Questions 21–27.

CANTERBURY COLLEGE

LIST OF COURSES

COURSE A
This course will enable students to experience performing arts and the media at a basic level. It will give them the experience to decide if they wish to pursue an interest in this field and to develop their potential and adaptability for working in a performance company in either a performing or a technical role.

COURSE B
The aim of this course is to provide a thorough grounding in business-related skills and a comprehensive knowledge of business practice. It is for students with a business studies background who can manage a heavy workload that will contain a greater degree of academic study.

COURSE C
This course provides progression to a range of higher levels. Units will include maintaining employment standards, salon management duties, providing facial massage and skin care, instruction on make-up, lash and brow treatments, artificial nail structures and ear piercing.

COURSE D
This course is designed to develop skills used in leisure operations. It covers preparing for and conducting physical activities, maintenance of facility areas, building relationships with participants and colleagues, handling sports equipment and health and safety issues.

COURSE E
This course gives a foundation for a career in caring for children, the elderly or people with special needs. Core units are Numeracy, Communication and Information Technology. Work placements are an important part of the course.

COURSE F
This course is designed to provide a foundation in graphic and visual communication skills. Students complete units in picture composition and photographic processing alongside elements of graphic design, and gain hands-on experience of desktop publishing and presentations.

COURSE G
This course is designed to provide an introduction to the construction industry. Units covered include Heat, Light and Sound, Introduction to the Urban Environment, Communication Processes and Techniques and Properties of Materials. All students complete vocational assignments which are integrated with work experience with reputable companies.

COURSE H
The qualifications gained and the skills developed on this course will provide a good basis for gaining employment in office work. In addition to word processing, the course also covers spreadsheets, computerised accounting, databases and desktop publishing. All students are given chances to develop their confidence, and advice and information is given on job search skills, presentation techniques and personal appearance.

Questions 21–27

*Look at the List of Courses at Canterbury College **A–H** on the previous page.*

Which course would you recommend for people with the following career interests?

*Write the correct letter **A–H** in boxes 21–27 on your answer sheet.*

21 advertising

22 TV production

23 architecture

24 company management

25 working with the disabled

26 secretarial tasks

27 beauty therapy

SECTION 3   *Questions 28–40*

Read the passage below and answer Questions 28–40.

The History of Early Cinema

The history of the cinema in its first thirty years is one of major and, to this day, unparalleled expansion and growth. Beginning as something unusual in a handful of big cities – New York, London, Paris and Berlin – the new medium quickly found its way across the world, attracting larger and larger audiences wherever it was shown and replacing other forms of entertainment as it did so. As audiences grew, so did the places where films were shown, finishing up with the 'great picture palaces' of the 1920s, which rivalled, and occasionally superseded, theatres and opera houses in terms of opulence and splendour. Meanwhile, films themselves developed from being short 'attractions' only a couple of minutes long, to the full-length feature that has dominated the world's screens up to the present day.

Although French, German, American and British pioneers have all been credited with the invention of cinema, the British and the Germans played a relatively small role in its world-wide exploitation. It was above all the French, followed closely by the Americans, who were the most passionate exporters of the new invention, helping to start cinema in China, Japan, Latin America and Russia. In terms of artistic development it was again the French and the Americans who took the lead, though in the years before the First World War, Italy, Denmark and Russia also played a part.

In the end, it was the United States that was to become, and remain, the largest single market for films. By protecting their own market and pursuing a vigorous export policy, the Americans achieved a dominant position on the world market by the start of the First World War. The centre of film-making had moved westwards, to Hollywood, and it was films from these new Hollywood studios that flooded onto the world's film markets in the years after the First World War, and have done so ever since. Faced with total Hollywood domination, few film industries proved competitive. The Italian industry, which had pioneered the feature film with spectacular films like *Quo vadis?* (1913) and *Cabiria* (1914), almost collapsed. In Scandinavia, the Swedish cinema had a brief period of glory, notably with powerful epic films and comedies. Even the French cinema found itself in a difficult position. In Europe, only Germany proved industrially capable, while in the new Soviet Union and in Japan the development of the cinema took place in conditions of commercial isolation.

Hollywood took the lead artistically as well as industrially. Hollywood films appealed because they had better-constructed narratives, their special effects were more impressive, and the star system added a new dimension to screen acting. If Hollywood did not have enough of its own resources, it had a great deal of money to buy up artists and technical innovations from Europe to ensure its continued dominance over present or future competition.

The rest of the world survived partly by learning from Hollywood and partly because audiences continued to exist for a product which corresponded to needs which Hollywood could not supply. As well as popular audiences, there were also increasing audiences for films which were artistically more adventurous or which dealt with the issues in the outer world.

None of this would have happened without technology, and cinema is in fact unique as an art form. In the early years, this art form was quite primitive, similar to the original French idea of using a lantern and slides back in the seventeenth century. Early cinema programmes were a mixture of items, combining comic sketches, free-standing narratives, serial episodes and the occasional trick or animated film. With the arrival of the feature-length narrative as the main attraction, other types of films became less important. The making of cartoons became a separate branch of film-making, generally practised outside the major studios, and the same was true of serials. Together with newsreels, they tended to be shown as short items in a programme which led to the feature.

From early cinema, it was only American slapstick comedy that successfully developed in both short and feature format. However, during this 'Silent Film' era, animation, comedy, serials and dramatic features continued to thrive, along with factual films or documentaries, which acquired an increasing distinctiveness as the period progressed. It was also at this time that the avant-garde film first achieved commercial success, this time thanks almost exclusively to the French and the occasional German film.

Of the countries which developed and maintained distinctive national cinemas in the silent period, the most important were France, Germany and the Soviet Union. Of these, the French displayed the most continuity, in spite of the war and post-war economic uncertainties. The German cinema, relatively insignificant in the pre-war years, exploded on to the world scene after 1919. Yet even they were both overshadowed by the Soviets after the 1917 Revolution. They turned their back on the past, leaving the style of the pre-war Russian cinema to the émigrés who fled westwards to escape the Revolution.

The other countries whose cinemas changed dramatically are: Britain, which had an interesting but undistinguished history in the silent period; Italy, which had a brief moment of international fame just before the war; the Scandinavian countries, particularly Denmark, which played a role in the development of silent cinema quite out of proportion to their small population; and Japan, where a cinema developed based primarily on traditional theatrical and, to a lesser extent, other art forms and only gradually adapted to western influence.

Questions 28–30

Choose **THREE** *letters A–F.*

Write your answers in boxes 28–30 on your answer sheet.

Which **THREE** possible reasons for American dominance of the film industry are given in the text?

    A   plenty of capital to purchase what it didn't have
    B   making films dealing with serious issues
    C   being first to produce a feature film
    D   well-written narratives
    E   the effect of the First World War
    F   excellent special effects

Questions 31–33

Answer the questions below using **NO MORE THAN THREE WORDS** *from the passage for each answer.*

Write your answers in boxes 31–33 on your answer sheet.

31   Which **TWO** types of film were not generally made in major studios?

32   Which type of film did America develop in both short and feature films?

33   Which type of film started to become profitable in the 'silent' period?

Questions 34–40

Look at the following statements (Questions 34–40) and the list of countries below.

Match each statement with the correct country.

Write the correct letter A–J in boxes 34–40 on your answer sheet.

NB You may use any letter more than once.

34　It helped other countries develop their own film industry.

35　It was the biggest producer of films.

36　It was first to develop the 'feature' film.

37　It was responsible for creating stars.

38　It made the most money from 'avant-garde' films.

39　It made movies based more on its own culture than outside influences.

40　It had a great influence on silent movies, despite its size.

List of Countries	
A　France	**F**　Japan
B　Germany	**G**　Soviet Union
C　USA	**H**　Italy
D　Denmark	**I**　Britain
E　Sweden	**J**　China

WRITING

WRITING TASK 1

You should spend about 20 minutes on this task.

> **You were hurt in a minor accident inside a supermarket, and you wish to complain to the supermarket.**
>
> **Write a letter to the manager of the supermarket. In your letter**
> - **say who you are**
> - **give details about the accident**
> - **suggest how the supermarket could prevent similar accidents.**

Write at least 150 words.

You do **NOT** need to write any addresses.

Begin your letter as follows:

Dear Sir or Madam,

WRITING TASK 2

You should spend about 40 minutes on this task.

Write about the following topic:

> **In the past, many people had skills such as making their own clothes and doing repairs to things in the house. In many countries, nowadays, skills like these are disappearing.**
>
> **Why do you think this change is happening?**
>
> **How far is this situation true in your country?**

Give reasons for your answer and include any relevant examples from your own knowledge or experience.

Write at least 250 words.

General Training: Reading and Writing Test B

READING

SECTION 1   *Questions 1–14*

Read the information below and answer Questions 1–7.

Booking a Wessex Cottages Holiday

How to book your holiday
When you have looked through our brochure and have chosen two or three alternative cottages you would like to stay in, please phone our Holiday Booking Office.

The number is: 01225 892299

31ˢᵗ March to 20ᵗʰ October
Monday, Tuesday, Wednesday, Friday 9.00 a.m. to 5.00 p.m. and Thursday 9.30 a.m. to 5.00 p.m.
Saturday Closed
Sunday Closed

21ˢᵗ October to 30ᵗʰ March
Monday, Tuesday, Wednesday, Friday 9.00 a.m. to 5.00 p.m. and Thursday 9.30 a.m. to 5.00 p.m.
Saturday 9.30 a.m. to 4.30 p.m.
Sunday Closed

We will check the availability of your choices and our reservation staff will help you make your decision. Should none of your choices be available, we will do our best to suggest suitable alternatives.

When a provisional reservation has been made, it will be held for 7 days. We will give you a holiday reference number and ask you to complete the holiday booking form and return it, with a deposit of ONE THIRD of the cottage rental, to:
WESSEX COTTAGES HOLIDAY BOOKING OFFICE
PO BOX 675
MELKSHAM
WILTSHIRE SN12 8SX
Deposit payments can be made by credit card at the time of booking or by cheque made payable to:
Wessex Cottages Ltd.

IF WE HAVE NOT RECEIVED YOUR COMPLETED AND SIGNED BOOKING FORM WITH DEPOSIT WITHIN 7 DAYS, WE REGRET THAT YOUR RESERVATION WILL BE CANCELLED.

When we receive your booking form and deposit, your reservation will be confirmed – we will send you a Booking Confirmation, together with advice on how to reach your holiday cottage and the telephone number of a local contact should you require further details on the cottage before leaving home. Attached to the Booking Confirmation will be a note showing the balance due on your holiday and the date by which it is payable. Outstanding balances on bookings made in the UK must be settled within 10 weeks of sending the deposit.

ARRIVAL
Please do not arrive at your holiday cottage before 3.30 p.m. or later than 7.00 p.m.

DEPARTURE
On the morning of departure, please leave your holiday property by 10 a.m. to allow caretakers sufficient time to prepare the property for the next visitors. We ask that you please leave the property as you found it. Please do not move the furniture as this can cause damage both to the furniture and to the property.

OVERSEAS BOOKINGS
We are delighted to take bookings from overseas visitors either by telephone or fax + 44 (0)1225 890227. All payments should be made by credit card

or by cheque in Pounds Sterling. Please note that provisional bookings from overseas visitors will be held for 14 DAYS. If the completed and signed booking form with the deposit is not received within that time, the reservation will be cancelled.

LAST-MINUTE BOOKINGS
If you wish to make a last-minute booking, please telephone the Holiday Booking Office to check availability.

If your reservation is made within 10 weeks of the holiday start date, full payment is due on booking.

ELECTRICITY
In most Wessex Cottages properties electricity must be paid for in addition to the holiday price. You may be asked to take a meter reading at the conclusion of your holiday, or an additional fixed charge for electricity may be made. Alternatively, there may be a coin meter, in which case you will be advised when you are making your booking. In some cottages, electricity is included in the rental and in very few there is no electricity at all.

LINEN
In most Wessex Cottages properties you have the choice either of hiring linen, at a cost of £6.00 per person per week, or of bringing your own. In some cottages linen is included and in a very few it is not available at all. If you choose to hire linen, it will include bed linen (i.e. sheets and/or duvet covers and pillow cases), bath and hand towels and tea cloths but will not include towels for swimming or beach use. Linen is not available for cots. If you have any queries, do ask the Holiday Booking Office.

Questions 1–7

Look at the information above about renting holiday cottages in England.

Do the following statements agree with the information given in the passage?

In boxes 1–7 on your answer sheet write

TRUE	*if the statement agrees with the information*
FALSE	*if the statement contradicts the information*
NOT GIVEN	*if there is no information on this*

1   The office is open on Saturdays in February but closes slightly earlier than on weekdays.

2   On receipt of your deposit, Wessex Cottages will confirm your booking by telephone.

3   For UK bookings, any outstanding balance must be paid within ten weeks of sending the deposit.

4   Between the departure of one visitor and the arrival of the next, the properties are visited and made ready.

5   The cost is lower if you make a last-minute booking.

6   Electricity is included in the rental of the majority of Wessex Cottages properties.

7   Beach towels are available for hire.

Read the advertisements below and answer Questions 8–14.

A

STEADMAN & CO
CHARTERED ACCOUNTANTS

**All professional services, including
Auditing, Accountancy and
Taxation from Small
Businesses to Large Corporations.**

Personal attention given at all times.

**12, Church Street, Ely
Telephone: (01353) 562547/561331**

B

St Paul's Garage (Ely)

Full Mechanical and Body Repair Service

Insurance Company Approved
Resprays and Restorations
Breakdown Service

**6, River Lane, Ely, Cambs CB6 4BU
Telephone: Ely 552247**

C

Accident
Victim?

Injured in an accident? Was someone
else at fault? Find out free from a
specialist solicitor if you can claim
compensation.

Call:
Freephone 0800 8760831 (24 hours)
National Accident Helpline

D

MELROSE BUFFET CATERING

**Professional Caterers with 15 years'
experience**

BEFORE YOU BOOK A FUNCTION LET US
GIVE YOU A QUOTE. WE WILL SUPPLY THE
BEST WITHIN YOUR STATED BUDGET. WE CATER
FOR SMALL OR LARGE FUNCTIONS, IN YOUR HOME,
OFFICE, GARDEN, TOWN HALL, CHURCH HALL,
IN FACT ANYWHERE YOU WISH.

**"YOU SUPPLY THE VENUE, WE WILL SUPPLY
THE MENU" – A MENU TO SUIT
YOUR BUDGET.**

**28, Bury Road, Milton,
Cambridge. Telephone 01223 640789**

E

L M Limo Hire

**Private Hire Cars for Weddings
and Special Occasions etc.**

John & Sue Bishop

The White House, 12A Fair Street,
Ely CB6 1AE

Telephone: 01353 667184

F

**AIR TICKETS
EXPRESS ✈**

Your hotline to the **world**

If you are serious about booking
a flight anywhere in the world
and a reliable service is as
important as a cheap price ...
CALL US NOW

0990 320321

25, Union Road, Bishops Stortford,
Herts CM23 2LY

Questions 8–14

*Look at the twelve advertisements for local businesses **A–L** on the previous pages.*

Which business should be contacted in each of the following situations?

*Write the correct letter **A–L** in boxes 8–14 on your answer sheet.*

8   I have had an accident in my car. One of the rear lights is broken. I need to have it replaced.

9   I am helping to organise a wedding. The party will be at the bride's family's house but we are looking for someone to provide the food.

10   I have just found a house that I want to buy and I need a lawyer to help me with all the paperwork.

11   I have just returned from a holiday in Thailand, where I bought a Thai recipe book. I want to use the recipes in my restaurant, but I need someone to help me understand them.

12   I have just got a new job. I need to find somewhere to live locally.

13   Some friends are coming to visit me for the weekend, but my house is too small to put them all up. I want to find somewhere for them to stay.

14   I work in a local firm of solicitors. It's nearly the end of the tax year and I am trying to find someone to help us organise our finances.

SECTION 2   *Questions 15–27*

Read the passage below and answer Questions 15–21.

Courses Available at North Coast College Campuses

Agriculture

Specialist agriculture centres of the North Coast College offer courses ranging from agricultural skills to beef production, horse studies and rural management. The Wollongbar Campus is renowned for its Tropical Fruit Growing program and has introduced modules on macadamias, bushfoods and coffee production. Taree offers the Veterinary Assistant program and has introduced 'Agristudy', which enables students to learn flexibly and by correspondence, using a mixture of student learning guides, telephone tutorials, information sessions and workshops. Mullumbimby has the popular Rural Business Management program, which can also be studied by correspondence. Grafton, meanwhile, offers traineeships in agriculture including Beef and Dairy.

Health programs

The continued promotion of healthier living within the community has seen an increase in fitness awareness and a need for trained staff in the Fitness and Sport industries. Fitness Instruction courses are offered at Tweed Heads and teach students how to put together and lead a safe fitness program.

Lismore offers the Aged Support program and Port Macquarie offers the Early Childhood Nursing program. These courses give you the theoretical skills, knowledge and practical experience needed to work in a variety of residential and community-based health care institutions. For students interested in working in the Remedial Health Care industry, Kingscliff is a specialist centre for the Natural Therapy Diploma and has a health clinic on campus.

Environmental Studies

The Environmental Studies courses offered by the North Coast College have been developed to help students increase their awareness and understanding of environmental issues and to enable them to determine their environmental impact. The Environmental Practice course, which includes Coastal Management, is offered through Ballina campus.

For people interested in working to restore degraded natural forests, the North Coast College offers the Forest Regeneration course at Casino. This course can provide a pathway for students into the Natural Resource Management Diploma at university. Marine Industry Management programs are offered at Coffs Harbour.

Questions 15–21

Look at the following list of campuses (Questions 15–21) and the fields of study below.

Match each campus with the field of study available there.

Write the correct letter A–K in boxes 15–21 on your answer sheet.

15   Wollongbar

16   Grafton

17   Tweed Heads

18   Lismore

19   Port Macquarie

20   Ballina

21   Coffs Harbour

Fields of Study
A   forest restoration
B   banana cultivation
C   horse breeding
D   infant illness
E   elderly care
F   fish farming
G   herbal therapy
H   cattle farming
I   beach protection
J   animal health
K   recreation programs

Read the passage below and answer Questions 22–27.

Information on Photocopying

Information Services provide a Prepaid Services Card system for student and staff use of photocopiers and associated equipment in the Library, and use of laser printers in B Block. The same system has recently been installed in the Student Representative Council (SRC) for use with photocopiers there.

The system uses a plastic card similar to a keycard. Each card, called a 'Prepaid Services Card', has a unique, six-digit account number that accesses the system. Initially, students and other users will have to purchase a Prepaid Services Card from a teller machine located in the Library or B Block Computer Labs. The Prepaid Services Card costs $2.00. It is important that you keep a record of your card's account number and sign your name or write your student ID number on the card.

Users prepay for Library, Computer Lab or SRC services by adding value to their Prepaid Services Card. There are no refunds, so only add value for the amount of prepaid services you intend to use. The maximum amount of prepaid services or value that can be added to a card is $50.00.

Two note and coin teller machines have been installed, one in the photocopy room on Level 2 of the Library and the other in the B Block Computer Labs. These teller machines accept any denomination of coins or notes up to $50.00. The SRC has a smaller, coin only, teller machine.

When a new card is purchased, the Library and B Block Computer Labs teller machines automatically issue a receipt to the user. However, when adding credit to your existing card the printing of receipts is optional.

For added security, a card user may choose to allocate a PIN or Personal Identification Number to their Prepaid Services Card. The PIN must then be entered each time the card is used.

Questions 22–27

Do the following statements agree with the information given in the passage on the previous page?

In boxes 22–27 on your answer sheet write

> **TRUE** *if the statement agrees with the information*
> **FALSE** *if the statement contradicts the information*
> **NOT GIVEN** *if there is no information on this*

22   Prepaid Services Cards are in use in three locations.

23   You can only buy a Prepaid Services Card at the Library.

24   The smallest amount that can be added to the Prepaid Services Card at the Library teller machine is $5.

25   The Prepaid Services Card can be used to pay library fines.

26   Notes and coins can be used in all teller machines.

27   A PIN is allocated when you purchase your Prepaid Services Card.

SECTION 3   *Questions 28–40*

Questions 28–34

The passage on the following pages has seven sections **A–G**.

Choose the correct heading for each section from the list of headings below.

*Write the correct number **i–x** in boxes 28–34 on your answer sheet.*

List of Headings
i   Bee behaviour is a mystery
ii   Communicating direction when outside a hive
iii   How bees carry food on their bodies
iv   Von Frisch discovers that bees communicate
v   How bees communicate direction when inside a hive
vi   The special position of bee language
vii   Expressing distance by means of dance
viii   The purpose of the two simple dances
ix   The discovery that bees have a special scent
x   Von Frisch discovers three types of dance

28   Section **A**

29   Section **B**

30   Section **C**

31   Section **D**

32   Section **E**

33   Section **F**

34   Section **G**

Understanding Bee Behaviour

A

A bee's brain is the size of a grass seed, yet in this tiny brain are encoded some of the most complex and amazing behavioural patterns witnessed outside humankind. For bees are arguably the only animals apart from humans which have their own language. Earlier this century Karl von Frisch, a professor of Zoology at Munich University, spent decades of 'the purest joy of discovery' unravelling the mysteries of bee behaviour. For his astonishing achievements he was awarded the Nobel Prize and it is from his work that most of today's knowledge of what bees say to each other derives.

B

It started simply enough. Von Frisch knew from experiments by an earlier researcher that if he put out a bowl of sweet sugar syrup, bees might at first take some time to find it but, once they had done so, within the hour, hundreds of other bees would be eagerly taking the syrup. Von Frisch realised that, in some way, messages were being passed on back at the hive[1], messages which said, 'Out there, at this spot, you're going to find food.'

C

But how was it happening? To watch the bees, von Frisch constructed a glass-sided hive. He found that, once the scout bees arrived back at the hive, they would perform one of three dance types. In the first type, a returning scout scampered in circles, alternating to right and left, stopping occasionally to regurgitate food samples to the excited bees chasing after her. In the second dance, clearly an extended version of this round dance, she performed a sickle-shaped figure-of-eight pattern instead. In the third, distinctly different dance, she started by running a short distance in a straight line, waggling her body from side to side, and returning in a semi-circle to the starting point before repeating the process. She also stopped from time to time to give little bits of food to begging bees. Soon the others would excitedly leave the hive in search of food. Minutes later, many of them, marked by von Frisch, could be seen eating at the bowls of sugar syrup.

---

1. Hive – a 'house' for bees; the place where they build a nest and live

D

Experimenting further, von Frisch unravelled the mystery of the first two related types, the round and the sickle dances. These dances, he concluded, told the bees simply that, within quite short distances of the hive there was a food source worth chasing. The longer and more excitedly the scout danced, the richer the promise of the food source. The scent she carried in her samples and on her body was a message to the other bees that this particular food was the one they were looking for. The others would then troop out of the hive and fly in spiralling circles 'sniffing' in the wind for the promised food.

E

At first, von Frisch thought the bees were responding only to the scent of the food. But what did the third dance mean? And if bees were responding only to the scent, how could they also 'sniff down' food hundreds of metres away from the hive, food which was sometimes downwind? On a hunch, he started gradually moving the feeding dish further and further away and noticed as he did so, that the dances of the returning scout bees also started changing. If he placed the feeding dish over nine metres away, the second type of dance, the sickle version, came into play. But once he moved it past 36 metres, the scouts would then start dancing the third, quite different, waggle dance.

The measurement of the actual distance too, he concluded, was precise. For example, a feeding dish 300 metres away was indicated by 15 complete runs through the pattern in 30 seconds. When the dish was moved to 60 metres away, the number dropped to 11.

F

Von Frisch noted something further. When the scout bees came home to tell their sisters about the food source, sometimes they would dance outside on the horizontal entrance platform of the hive, and sometimes on the vertical wall inside. And, depending on where they danced, the straight portion of the waggle dance would point in different directions. The outside dance was fairly easy to decode: the straight portion of the dance pointed directly to the food source, so the bees would merely have to decode the distance message and fly off in that direction to find their food.

G

But by studying the dance on the inner wall of the hive, von Frisch discovered a remarkable method which the dancer used to tell her sisters the direction of the food in relation to the sun. When inside the hive, the dancer cannot use the sun, so she uses gravity instead. The direction of the sun is represented by the top of the hive wall. If she runs straight up, this means that the feeding place is in the same direction as the sun. However, if, for example, the feeding place is 40° to the left of the sun, then the dancer would run 40° to the left of the vertical line. This was to be the first of von Frisch's remarkable discoveries. Soon he would also discover a number of other remarkable facts about how bees communicate and, in doing so, revolutionise the study of animal behaviour generally.

Questions 35–37

*The writer mentions **THREE** kinds of bee dance identified by von Frisch.*

List the name the writer gives to each dance.

*Use **ONE WORD ONLY** for each answer.*

Write your answers in boxes 35–37 on your answer sheet.

35   ....

36   ....

37   ....

Questions 38–40

Look at the passage about bee behaviour on the previous pages.

Complete the sentences below with words taken from the passage.

*Write **NO MORE THAN THREE WORDS** for each answer.*

Write your answers in boxes 38–40 on your answer sheet.

38   Von Frisch discovered the difference between dance types by changing the position of ....

39   The dance outside the hive points in the direction of ....

40   The angle of the dance from the vertical shows the angle of the food from ....

WRITING

WRITING TASK 1

You should spend about 20 minutes on this task.

> *You want to sell some of your furniture. You think a friend of yours might like to buy it from you.*
>
> *Write a letter to your friend. In your letter*
>
> * *explain why you are selling*
> * *describe the furniture*
> * *suggest a date when your friend can come and see the furniture*

Write at least 150 words.

You do **NOT** need to write any addresses.

Begin your letter as follows:

Dear .... ,

WRITING TASK 2

You should spend about 40 minutes on this task.

Write about the following topic:

> *Some people believe that children should be allowed to stay at home and play until they are six or seven years old. Others believe that it is important for young children to go to school as soon as possible.*
>
> *What do you think are the advantages of attending school from a young age?*

Give reasons for your answer and include any relevant examples from your own knowledge or experience.

Write at least 250 words.

Tapescripts

SECTION 1

MAN: Good morning.
WOMAN: Good morning. How can I help you?
MAN: I understand that the school organises . . . umm, trips to different . . .
WOMAN: Yes, we run <u>five every month</u>: three during weekends and two Wednesday   *Example*
          afternoon trips.
MAN: What sort of places?
WOMAN: Well, obviously it varies, but always places of historical interest and also which
          offer a <u>variety of shopping</u>, because our students always ask about that . . . and   *Q1*
          then we go for ones where we know there are <u>guided tours</u>, because this gives a   *Q2*
          good focus for the visit.
MAN: Do you travel far?
WOMAN: Well, we're lucky here, obviously, because we're able to say that all our visits are
          less than three hours drive.
MAN: How much do they cost?
WOMAN: Again it varies – between five and fifteen pounds a head, depending on distance.
MAN: Ah ha . . .
WOMAN: Oh, and we do offer to arrange special trips if, you know, there are <u>more than</u>   *Q3*
          <u>twelve</u> people.
MAN: Oh right, I'll keep that in mind. And what are the times normally?
WOMAN: We try to keep it pretty fixed so that, that students get to know the pattern. We
          leave at eight-thirty a.m. and return at six p.m. We figure it's best to keep the day
          fairly short.
MAN: Oh yes. And how do we reserve a place?
WOMAN: You sign your name on the <u>notice board</u>. Do you know where it is?   *Q4*
MAN: Ah ha. I saw it this morning.
WOMAN: And we do ask that you sign up three days in advance so we know we've got
          enough people interested to run it, and we can cancel if necessary, with full refund
          of course.
MAN: That's fine, thanks.

MAN: And what visits are planned for this term?
WOMAN: Right, well I'm afraid the schedule hasn't been printed out yet, but we have
          confirmed the dates and planned the optional extra visits which you can also
          book in advance if you want to.
MAN: Oh that's all right. If you can just give some idea of the weekend ones so I can,
          you know, work out when to see friends, etcetera.

WOMAN:	Oh sure. Well, the first one is St Ives. That's on <u>the thirteenth of February</u> and we'll have only sixteen places available 'cos we're going by minibus. And that's a day in town with the optional extra of visiting the Hepworth Museum.	*Q5*
MAN:	Oh right . . . yeah . . . that sounds good.	
WOMAN:	Then there's a London trip on the sixteenth of February and we'll be taking a medium-sized coach so there'll be forty-five places on that, and, let's see, the optional extra is the <u>Tower of London</u>.	*Q6*
MAN:	Oh, I've already been there.	
WOMAN:	After that there's <u>Bristol</u> on the third of March.	*Q7*
MAN:	Where?	
WOMAN:	Bristol . . . B-R-I-S-T-O-L.	
MAN:	OK . . .	
WOMAN:	That's in a different minibus with eighteen places available, oh, and the optional extra is a visit to the S.S. *Great Britain*.	
MAN:	OK . . .	
WOMAN:	We're going to Salisbury on the eighteenth of March and that's always a popular one because the optional extra is Stonehenge, so we're taking the large coach with fifty seats . . .	
MAN:	Oh good.	
WOMAN:	And then the last one is to Bath on the twenty-third of March.	
MAN:	Oh yes. Is Bath the Roman city?	
WOMAN:	Yes, that's right, and that's in the sixteen-seater minibus.	
MAN:	And where's the optional visit?	
WOMAN:	It's to the <u>American Museum</u> – well worth a visit.	*Q8*
MAN:	OK, well that's great, thanks for all that . . .	
WOMAN:	My pleasure. By the way, if you want more information about any of the trips, have a look in the <u>student newspaper</u>.	*Q9*
MAN:	OK.	
WOMAN:	Or, have a word with my assistant; her name is Jane <u>Yentob</u> – that's Y-E-N-T-O-B.	*Q10*
MAN:	Right, I've got that. Thank you very much for all your help.	
WOMAN:	You're very welcome. I hope you enjoy the trips.	

SECTION 2

Good afternoon everybody and welcome to Riverside Industrial Village. To start your visit I'm just going to give you a brief account of the history of the museum before letting you roam about on your own. I won't keep you long. OK?

Now, from where we're standing you've got a good view of the river over there. And it was because of this fast-flowing water that this site was a natural place for manufacturing works. The water and the availability of raw materials in the area, like minerals and iron ore, and also the abundance of local fuels, like <u>coal and firewood</u>, all made this site suitable for industry from a very early time. *Q11*

Water was the main source of power for the early industries and some of the water wheels

were first established in the twelfth century, would you believe? At that time, <u>local craftsmen</u> *Q12*
first built an iron forge just behind the village here, on the bend in the river. By the
seventeenth and eighteenth centuries the region's rivers supported more than <u>a hundred and</u> *Q13*
<u>sixty</u> water mills – and many of these continued to operate well into the nineteenth century.
But then the steam engine was invented and then the railways came and the centres of
industry were able to move away from the rivers and the countryside and into the towns. So,
industrial villages like this one became very rare.

So that's the history for you. If you'd like any more information, you can ask me some
questions, or you can read further in our excellent guide book.

Now I'm going to give you a plan of the site and I'd just like to point out where everything
is and then you can take a look at everything for yourself.

I've already pointed out the river, which is on the left. And of course, running along the
bottom is <u>Woodside</u> Road, got it? OK. Now we're standing at the entrance, see it at the *Q14*
bottom, and immediately to our right is the <u>Ticket Office</u>. You won't need that because *Q15*
you've got your group booking, but just past it are the toilets – always good to know where
they are. In front of us is the car park, as you can see, and to the left, by the entry gate is the
<u>Gift Shop</u>. That's where you can get copies of the guide, like this one here. *Q16*

Now, beyond the car park all the buildings are arranged in a half circle with a yard in the
middle. The big, stone building at the top is the <u>main Workshop</u>. That's where the furnace is *Q17*
and where all the metal was smelted and the tools were cast, as you'll be able to see. Now, in
the top right-hand corner, that building with bigger windows is the <u>Showroom</u>, where *Q18*
samples of all the tools that were made through the ages are on display. In the top left
corner is the Grinding Shop, where the tools were sharpened and finished. And on one side
of that you can see the Engine Room and on the other is the <u>Café</u>, which isn't an antique, *Q19*
you'll be pleased to know, though they do serve very nice old-fashioned teas.

The row of buildings you can see on the left are the <u>cottages</u>. These were built for the *Q20*
workers towards the end of the eighteenth century and they're still furnished from that
period so you can get a good idea of ordinary people's living conditions. Across the yard
from them, you can see the stables where the horses were kept for transporting the products.
And the separate building in front of them is the Works Office and that still has some of the
old accounts on display.

Right, if anyone wants a guided tour then I'm starting at the Engine Room. If you'd like to
come along, this way please, ladies and gentlemen.

SECTION 3

MELANIE: Excuse me, Dr Johnson. May I speak to you for a minute?
DR JOHNSON: Sure. Come in.
MELANIE: I'm Melanie Griffin. I'm taking your course in Population Studies.
DR JOHNSON: Right. Well, Melanie, how can I help you?
MELANIE: I'm . . . having a bit of trouble with the second assignment, and it's due in
                         twelve days.
DR JOHNSON: What sort of trouble are you having? Is the assignment question a problem?

MELANIE:	Well, that's part of the problem. I'm also having – been having – trouble getting hold of the books. I've been to the library several times, and all the books are out.	
DR JOHNSON:	Sounds like you should have started borrowing books a bit earlier.	
MELANIE:	Well, I had <u>a really big assignment due in for another course</u>, and I've been spending all my time on that, and I thought . . .	*Q21*
DR JOHNSON:	. . . you might get an extension of time to finish your assignment for me?	
MELANIE:	If that's possible, but I don't know . . .	
DR JOHNSON:	Well, yes, it is possible, but extensions are normally given only for <u>medical or compassionate reasons</u>, otherwise it's really a question of organising your study, and we don't like giving extensions to students who simply didn't plan their work properly. What did you get for your first assignment?	*Q22*
MELANIE:	I got eighty-seven per cent.	
DR JOHNSON:	Mmm, yes, you did very well indeed, so obviously you can produce good work.	
MELANIE:	I don't think I'll need too much extra time, as long as I can get hold of some of the important references.	
DR JOHNSON:	Well, since you did so well in your first assignment, I'm prepared to give you an extra two weeks for this one, so that'll mean you'll need to submit it about a month from now.	
MELANIE:	Thank you.	
DR JOHNSON:	Now, what about the reading materials? Have you checked out the journal articles in the list?	
MELANIE:	Umm, no, not yet, there were about twenty of them, and I wasn't sure which ones would be most useful or important.	
DR JOHNSON:	Well, they're all useful, but I don't expect anyone to read them all, because a number of them deal with the same issues. Let me give you some suggestions. The article by Anderson and Hawker is really worth reading.	
MELANIE:	Right, I'll read that one.	
DR JOHNSON:	You should also read the article by Jackson, but just look at the part on the <u>research methodology</u> – how they did it.	*Q23*
MELANIE:	OK . . . Jackson, got that . . .	
DR JOHNSON:	And if you have time, the one by Roberts says very relevant things, although it's not essential.	
MELANIE:	So, OK, if it's <u>useful</u>, I'll try and read that one . . .	*Q24*
DR JOHNSON:	Now, the one by Morris. I wouldn't bother with that at this stage, if I were you.	
MELANIE:	OK, I <u>won't bother</u> with Morris. Oh, now, someone told me the article by Cooper is important.	*Q25*
DR JOHNSON:	Well, yes, in a way, but just look at <u>the last part</u>, where he discusses the research results. And lastly, there's Forster – I can't think why I included that one. It's not bad and <u>could be of some help, but not that much</u>.	*Q26* *Q27*

DR JOHNSON:	Now, let's deal with the assignment question. What's the problem there?
MELANIE:	It's the graph on page two.

DR JOHNSON:	What seems to be the problem? It's just the bar graph showing reasons why people change where they live.
MELANIE:	Well, I've got a photocopy but the reasons at the bottom are missing.
DR JOHNSON:	OK. Look at the first bar on the graph – now that indicates the number of people who move because they want more space.
MELANIE:	Oh I see . . . bar one. OK . . . Now what about the next bar?
DR JOHNSON:	Bar two is to do with <u>the people living nearby disturbing them</u>, so they chose *Q28* to move away to somewhere quieter. Now let's look at bar number three . . . another reason people change their place of living is because they want to be closer to the city.
MELANIE:	OK. Proximity to the city is an issue . . .
DR JOHNSON:	Now . . . bar number four refers to problems when the owner of the property won't help fix things that go wrong. In other words, the <u>owner is not helpful</u> *Q29* and so the tenants move out.
MELANIE:	OK . . . now what about bar five?
DR JOHNSON:	Bar five is about those people who move because they need a bus or train to get them into the city or to go to work.
MELANIE:	OK . . . and bar six?
DR JOHNSON:	Bar number six is interesting. That reason was given quite a lot – people moving because they wanted to be in <u>a more attractive neighbourhood</u>. *Q30*
MELANIE:	Oh, yes, thank you very much.

SECTION 4

Good day, ladies and gentlemen. I have been asked today to talk to you about the urban landscape. There are two major areas that I will focus on in my talk: how vegetation can have a significant effect on urban climate, and how we can better plan our <u>cities using trees</u> *Q31* <u>to provide a more comfortable environment</u> for us to live in.

Trees can have a significant impact on our cities. They can make a city, as a whole, a bit less <u>windy</u> or a bit more windy, if that's what you want. They can make it a bit cooler if it's a hot *Q32* summer day in an Australian city, or they can make it a bit more <u>humid</u> if it's a dry inland *Q33* city. On the local scale – that is, in particular areas within the city – trees can make the local area more <u>shady</u>, cooler, more humid and much less windy. In fact trees and planting of *Q34* various kinds can be used to make city streets actually less <u>dangerous</u> in particular areas. *Q35* How do trees do all that, you ask?

Well, the main difference between a tree and a building is a tree has got an internal mechanism to keep the temperature regulated. It evaporates water through its <u>leaves</u> and *Q36* that means that the temperature of the leaves is never very far from our own body temperature. The temperature of a building surface on a hot sunny day can easily be twenty degrees more than our temperature. Trees, on the other hand, remain cooler than buildings because they sweat. This means that they can humidify the air and cool it – a property which can be exploited to improve the local climate.

Trees can also help break the force of winds. The reason that high buildings make it windier at <u>ground</u> level is that, as the wind goes higher and higher, it goes faster and faster. When the wind hits the building, it has to go somewhere. Some of it goes over the top and some goes around the sides of the building, forcing those high level winds down to ground level. That doesn't happen when you have trees. Trees <u>filter the wind and considerably reduce it</u>, preventing those very large strong gusts that you so often find around tall buildings. *Q37*

Q38

Another problem in built-up areas is that traffic noise is intensified by tall buildings. By planting a belt of trees at the side of the road, you can make things a little quieter, but much of the vehicle noise still goes through the trees. Trees can also help reduce the amount of noise in the surroundings, although the effect is not as large as people like to think. <u>Low-</u>frequency noise, in particular, just goes through the trees as though they aren't there. *Q39*

Although trees can significantly improve the local climate, they do however take up a lot of space. There are root systems to consider and branches blocking windows and so on. It may therefore be difficult to fit trees into the local landscape. There is not a great deal you can do if you have what we call a street canyon – a whole set of high-rises enclosed in a narrow street. Trees need water to grow. They also need some sunlight to grow and you <u>need room</u> to put them. If you have the chance of knocking buildings down and replacing them, then suddenly you can start looking at different ways to design the streets and to introduce . . . *(fade out)* *Q40*

TEST 2

SECTION 1

SALLY:	Oh, Peter, there you are. You've been ages. What kept you so long?
PETER:	I'm sorry I'm so late, Sally. Have you been waiting long?
SALLY:	Oh, <u>half an hour</u>. But it doesn't matter. I've had a coffee and I've been reading this guidebook for tourists. Sit down. You look very hot and tired. What would you like to drink?

Example

PETER:	I'd love a really <u>chilled mineral water</u> or something. Will you have another coffee?

Q1

SALLY:	Yes, I will. The waitress will be back in a moment. Why were you so late? Did something happen?
PETER:	Yes. You know I went to the bank to cash some travellers cheques? Well, the exchange rate was looking healthy, but when I went to the teller, they told me the <u>computer system was temporarily down</u>, so they couldn't do any transactions. They said the problem would be fixed in a few minutes, so I waited. And then I started talking to another guy in the bank, and I forgot the time.

Q2

SALLY:	Oh, really? Someone you met in the bank? Does he work there?
PETER:	No, he was <u>a tourist, from New York</u>. His name's Henry, and he's been here for a week, but he's moving on to Germany tomorrow. He's an architect, and he's spending four weeks travelling around Europe.

Q3

SALLY:	Just like us!
PETER:	Yeah, just like us. He told me the names of some places where we should eat. Great food, and not too expensive, he said. Oh, and he also gave me this map of <u>the bus system</u>. He said he didn't need it any more.

Q4

SALLY:	That's useful. Pity he's moving on tomorrow. Ah, here's the waitress. Let's order. Do you want anything to eat, or shall we just have a drink?
PETER:	Well, I'm hungry, and we've got a lot of sightseeing to do, so let's just have <u>a snack and a drink</u>.
SALLY:	Sounds good to me!

Q5

PETER:	Well, let's decide what we'll see today. I guess the best place to start is the Cathedral, and then the Castle. What are the opening times for those two?
SALLY:	Well, according to this guidebook, the Cathedral is only open from nine-thirty in the morning until midday. No, hang on. That's the Cathedral Museum. The <u>Cathedral itself is open morning</u> *and* <u>afternoon</u>. The Castle is just open from one to five, so we can't go there until after lunch. I really want to spend some time in the Art Gallery, because they've got this wonderful painting by Rembrandt that I've always wanted to see.
PETER:	What else should we see?
SALLY:	Well, the guidebook says the Botanical Gardens are worth spending some time in, and they're open all day, from eight to six, so we can go there any time. I'd like to go to the Markets near the river too, but . . . oh . . . no, wait, that's only in the mornings, too.
PETER:	As well as today and tomorrow, we can see some other places on Monday, you know. But <u>I don't think the Markets will be open then</u>; they only open on Thursdays, so we've missed them for this week. Maybe we should go to the Cathedral today because it's Sunday tomorrow, and even though it's open every day it might be more difficult to get in tomorrow because of the church services.
SALLY:	That's true, but the Art Gallery isn't open on Sundays at all, so we'll have to go there today. The Castle's open every day except Mondays, so we're OK there, and the Gardens of course only close at night.
PETER:	Are all these places free or do we have to pay to go in? What does the guidebook say?
SALLY:	I think there's <u>a charge for all of them except the Botanical Gardens</u>. Oh, and the Markets, of course you don't pay to go in.
PETER:	OK, well, it looks like our plan is this: <u>we'll go to see the painting you like first</u>, the Rembrandt, then have lunch and go on to the Castle after that, and then the Cathedral.
SALLY:	OK. It says here that the roof of the Cathedral is really beautiful.
PETER:	Is that right? What I really want to do at the Cathedral is <u>climb the tower</u>. The view is supposed to be spectacular.
SALLY:	OK, well, that'll be more than enough for today. Then, tomorrow, let's go to the Botanical Gardens and have a picnic. I want to sit by the river and watch the swans. This city's famous for them.

Q6

Q7

Q8

Q9

Q10

SECTION 2

So the counselling services we offer deal with any problems arising from your studies, or in your life outside the university. Let's take academic counselling. If you're confused about subjects or how to combine them in your degree, then we can advise you and discuss the career you are aiming for, so that you can see it all in context. We can also chase up your tutor if you're <u>not getting proper feedback on how you are getting on in your subject</u>. *Q11*

Besides help with academic problems, you may also need personal counselling: if you think you're already under stress, well, just wait till classes begin next week. You'll have to start adjusting to teaching and learning methods that may be unfamiliar to you, as well as the mounting pressure as the <u>deadline for that first assignment</u> creeps up on you. And of *Q12* course, you have to cope with all this without your usual social network – you know, the <u>social contacts, family and friends</u> you could normally rely on for help. All of this causes *Q13* anxiety. Studying overseas can trigger a personal crisis – you may have left a lot of what you might call 'unfinished business' back in your own country, or you may have <u>interrupted</u> *Q14* <u>personal relationships</u> or even sometimes have broken them off to come overseas, and so the student often feels lonely, unhappy, unmotivated and unable to concentrate on studying. Or there may be other things bothering you. Our resident chaplain can offer you spiritual guidance if that's what you want, or we can put you in touch with community groups that can provide you with social contacts and friendship.

What about exam stress? It affects nearly everyone to some extent, but especially overseas students like yourselves. There may be a huge amount of family pressure on you to succeed, and if you fail a subject or <u>drop out of a course</u> because it's too difficult then your self- *Q15* esteem can suffer. But it's not the end of the world if you don't pass an exam – I had to resit First Year Anthropology, so I can certainly offer you a sympathetic ear! Anyway, exam failure can lead to worrying changes in the way you normally behave. You may also be off your food, or you may have dietary problems because <u>the local food is not to your liking</u> *Q16* and upsets you, and this can affect your health and studies. Glenda Roberts is our dietician in the Health Service and we can put you on to her.

And we all have money problems, don't we? But remember, full-time students can get a low-interest loan of up to six hundred dollars <u>to buy books</u> and for similar study-related *Q17* expenses. That's right, and you can get double that amount if you can't afford an item of equipment you need for your course – a musical instrument, for example. And it doesn't stop there. When you move into a flat, starting-up expenses, including <u>furniture</u> for it, can be *Q18* covered by a loan through the Welfare Service – see Jill Freeman for details.

Can we help you? Well, last academic year, in spite of staff cuts, we counselled <u>two</u> *Q19* <u>hundred and forty</u> international students for a total of twenty-six hundred hours counselling, and, finally we won all but just one of the twelve appeals that we launched on behalf of students. Not too bad for <u>an understaffed service</u>, don't you think? That's all *Q20* from me. Thank you.

SECTION 3

ROSA: Oh, there you are, good. Sorry I'm a bit late – there was a long queue. So, have you worked out how to deal with this assignment then?

MICK: Not yet, we've only been here a couple of minutes ourselves.

ROSA: Can you just remind me what the task is exactly?

PETE: Well, there are two, no, three, parts to it: first, we've got to write an essay about ways of collecting data. Then . . .

ROSA: What's the title of the essay exactly?

MICK: I've got it here: 'Assess the two main methods of <u>collecting data</u> in social science research'.   *Q21*

ROSA: And how much do we need to write?

MICK: <u>Fifteen hundred</u> words. That's for the essay. Then, for the second part of the assignment, we have to choose one method of data collection, and 'carry out a small-scale study, making appropriate use of the method chosen to gather data from at least <u>five</u> subjects'.   *Q22*   *Q23*

ROSA: And then we have to write a report on the study?

PETE: That's right, of <u>three to four thousand</u> words.   *Q24*

ROSA: Did you get as far as discussing which form of data collection we should go for – questionnaire or interview, isn't it?

MICK: Yeah, I think we should use a questionnaire. It'll be so much less time-consuming than organising interviews, I reckon. Once we've agreed on the wording of it, we only have to send it out and wait for the responses.

ROSA: Yes, I think it probably would be quicker. But what did that article he gave us last week say about the quality of data from questionnaires?

MICK: I'm pretty sure it recommended questionnaires as a source of 'highly reliable data'. As long as you design the questionnaire properly in the first place, the data will be fine.

ROSA: No, I'm sure it talked about drawbacks as well, didn't it? Something about the <u>response rate</u> and the problems you get if it's too low.   *Q25*

MICK: Yeah, but we only need data from five subjects anyway.

ROSA: I suppose so. Another drawback I remember it mentioned was that questionnaire data <u>tends not to reveal anything unexpected</u>, because it is limited to the questions fixed in advance by the researcher.   *Q26*

MICK: Come on, Rosa. This is only a practice. It's not meant to be real research, is it?

ROSA: Well, I'm not sure about that.

- -

ROSA: Maybe I'd better go through the article again, just to be sure. Can you remember what it was called?

MICK: 'Sample Surveys in Social Science Research', I think. By <u>Mehta</u>.   *Q27*

ROSA: M-E-H-T-A ?

MICK: Yeah. And he also recommended a more recent book, called '<u>Survey Research</u>', by Bell, I think. It's in that series published by <u>London University</u>.   *Q28*   *Q29*

PETE: And if we tried to use interviews instead, I saw a book in the departmental library that'll be helpful: it's called 'Interviews that work', by Wilson, published in Oxford in <u>nineteen eighty-eight</u>.   *Q30*

ROSA: Right. I've got a tutorial now. Can we meet up again later this week? What about Friday morning?

PETE: Suits me. Eleven o'clock?

ROSA: Fine.

MICK: Before Friday, I think we should all look through the reading list.

SECTION 4

So far, in these lectures, we've been looking at crimes like robbery and murder – both from a historical viewpoint and also in contemporary society – and we've seen that the preoccupation in Western society with crime and with lawlessness is part of a long and continuous tradition, rather than something which is new and unique to modern society.

But over the past seventy years or so, there has been a massive increase in one type of crime, which is what's known as 'corporate crime'. Corporate crime is crime which, as the name suggests, is connected with companies, with business organisations. It includes illegal   *Q31*
acts of either individuals or a group within the company, but what is important is that these acts are normally in accordance with the goals of the company – they're for the good of the company rather than the individual. It's been defined as, quote, 'crime which is committed for the corporate organisation' – the company – 'not against it', unquote.

So crimes like theft by employees – things like embezzlement or fraud against one's   *Q32*
actual employer are excluded according to this definition. The employees may be involved but they're acting in the first place for the company – they may not even realise they're committing a crime or they may realise but they feel it's excusable because it's policy, or because otherwise they may lose their jobs. So here, really, we're talking about the links between power and crime.

Now, this is one area that much less is generally known about than conventional or traditional crime. It has been relatively ignored by the mass media – for example, it tends to   *Q33*
be under-reported in comparison with conventional crime in news broadcasts, and in crime serials and films and so on – they very rarely deal with corporate crime. And it also tends to be ignored in academic circles – there's been far more research on conventional crime and   *Q34*
far more data is available.

There are several reasons for this lack of interest in corporate crime, compared with other types of crime. It's often very complex, whereas with conventional crime it's usually possible to follow what's going on without specialist knowledge. As well as this, whereas   *Q35*
conventional crime usually has a lot of human interest, corporate crime often has much less. The third reason, and possibly the most significant one, is that very often the victims are unaware – they think their misfortune is an accident or that it's the fault of no-one in   *Q36*
particular. They're unaware that they've been victims of a crime.

So, when we look at the effects of corporate crime we may find it's very difficult to assess the costs. But these costs can be very considerable in both their economic and social aspects.

Let's look at the economic costs first. For example, if a company is producing fruit juice and it dilutes its product so that it's just a little below the concentration it should be, many millions of people may be paying a small amount extra for their carton of orange juice. Now small amounts like this may seem insignificant for individual customers – too small to   *Q37*
worry about – but for the company this deception might result in massive illegal profit.   *Q38*
However, all studies of corporate crime agree that the individuals are in fact deprived of far more money by such crime than they are by conventional crime like robbery and theft.

In addition to this, we have to consider the social costs of corporate crime and these are again very difficult to assess, but they are considerable. They're important because they can undermine the faith of the public in the business world and also, more importantly, because the main group of people they affect are, in fact, not the richer sections of society but the poorer – so here companies are robbing the poor to benefit the rich.

There are two more points to do with corporate crime that I'd like to illustrate with reference to a specific event which occurred several years ago. This was an explosion of a large oil tanker which caused the loss of more than fifty lives of the crew. It was an explosion which never should have happened and a subsequent inquiry laid the blame not on anyone who had actually been on the tanker at the time, but on the owners of the tanker. They had deliberately decided not to carry out necessary repair work on the tanker as it was due to be sold, and it was this lack of repair work which was directly responsible for the explosion.

Now this illustrates two points to do with corporate crime. First of all, that it does not have to be intentional. The owners of the tanker certainly did not intend it to explode. But very serious consequences can result from people or organisations not considering the possible results of their actions seriously enough. The main crime here was <u>indifference to the human results rather than actual intention to harm anyone, but that didn't make the results any less tragic</u>.

Q39 & Q40

And this leads me to my second point – that corporate crime can have very severe consequences. It's not just a matter of companies making bigger profits than they should do, but of events which may affect the lives of innocent people, and yet very often companies, because they say they didn't intend to harm anyone, can avoid taking responsibility for the results of their actions. And that has been a very dangerous loophole in the law.

A further example of corporate crime was . . . *(fade out)*

TEST 3

SECTION 1

LYNDA: Sara, I've heard that you want to move into a homestay family. Is that correct?

SARA: Yes, that's right. I've been staying with my aunt and now my cousin is arriving from Singapore and my aunt needs the room for him.

LYNDA: Oh, that's bad luck. Well, I'll need to get some particulars first. Sara, what's your full name?

SARA: <u>Sara Lim</u>, and that's Sara without the 'h' at the end.   *Example*

LYNDA: Mmm. How old are you, Sara?

SARA: Twenty-three, only just. It was my birthday on the twenty-first of August.

LYNDA: Happy Birthday for yesterday. How long have you been in Australia?

SARA: <u>A year in Adelaide and six months in Sydney</u>. I prefer Sydney, I've got more friends here.   *Q1*

LYNDA: What's your address at your aunt's house?

SARA: Flat one, five three nine <u>Forest</u> Road, Canterbury. And the post code is two, o, three, six.   *Q2*

LYNDA: OK. What are you studying now?

SARA: I was studying General English in Adelaide and now I'm doing <u>Academic</u> English, because I'm trying to get into Medicine next year.   *Q3*

LYNDA:	That sounds good, but it'll take you a long time. When would you like to move out from your aunt's?
SARA:	My cousin arrives on Friday morning, so I'd better be out on <u>Thursday</u>.
LYNDA:	What, the seventh of September?
SARA:	Yes, that's right.

Q4

LYNDA:	That doesn't leave us much time. Right, OK. I need to know what kind of accommodation you'd like, so I can get you something suitable.
SARA:	Can I <u>share a room</u> with someone else? I've been alone in my room at my aunt's and I've always shared with my sister and I like that.
LYNDA:	Yes, fine. That'll save you money too. Would you like to live with a family or do you think that a <u>single person</u> would be better for you? I have lots of very nice single people on my books.
SARA:	Do you have any women living alone, retired women?
LYNDA:	Yes, I have quite a few whose children have grown up and left home. In fact, I have some really lovely retired ladies, living by themselves, who just love the company of students. Most of them live in <u>flats</u>, but that's not a problem for you, is it?
SARA:	Not at all. I'm used to that. My aunt lives in a flat too, remember. I'm not used to a big house with a garden, swimming pool, pets and all that.
LYNDA:	OK, fine. I know quite a bit about what you want now. I should let you know that your rent will be a hundred and sixty dollars per week. You'll have to pay me three hundred and twenty dollars as a <u>deposit</u> before you move in. The deposit is as insurance, in case you break something. You'll need to pay <u>monthly</u> to me, by cash or cheque, I don't mind. You don't need to pay for gas, electricity or water, but you will need to pay your proportion of the <u>phone</u> bill. Most families do that on an honour system, but you'll have to wait and see.
SARA:	Mmm.
LYNDA:	Have you got any more questions for me?
SARA:	When will you know where I can go?
LYNDA:	I'll work on it now, so come and see me tomorrow and I should have some news for you then.
SARA:	Thanks a lot.
LYNDA:	Goodbye. See you tomorrow – after lunch would be better for me.
SARA:	OK, see you then. Bye.

Q5
Q6
Q7
Q8
Q9
Q10

SECTION 2

GEOFFREY:	Good evening, and in this week's edition of 'Focus on the Arts', Jane Hemmington is going to fill us in on what's in store for us at this year's Summer Festival. Over to you, Jane.
JANE:	Thank you, Geoffrey. This year, the Summer Festival is the biggest we've ever seen, so there should be something for everybody. This is the third year they've run it and the timing's slightly different: for the last couple of years

it's been around the fifth to seventeenth, but this year they wanted to allow everyone enough time to recover from the first of January celebrations and they've put it <u>at the end of the month</u>.   *Q11*

The programme has sensational theatre, dance and also a large number of art exhibitions, but the thing the Festival is most famous for is its great street music. For today's report though, Geoffrey, I'm looking at some of the <u>theatrical events</u> that you might like to see; in particular, at this year's theme – circuses.   *Q12*

I'm going to tell you about two circus performances, but there are <u>plenty</u> <u>of others in the programme</u>. I've chosen these because they represent distinct movements within circus performance. The first is the *Circus Romano* from Italy. As this is a travelling circus, it follows a long tradition by performing <u>in a marquee</u> – which is really like a canvas portable building, usually put up in a green space or car park, rather than in a theatre or stadium.   *Q13*   *Q14*

In spite of this, *Circus Romano* isn't at all like the traditional circuses I grew up with. There are no animals – just very talented clowning and acrobatic routines. The show has a lot of very funny moments, especially at the beginning, but the best part is the music and <u>lighting</u>. They're magical. At forty-five dollars it's very expensive anyway – it's really for <u>adult</u> tastes. In fact, much of it would be wasted on children – so I suggest you leave them at home.   *Q15*   *Q16*

The second circus performance is *Circus Electrica* at the <u>Studio Theatre</u>. The purists are suggesting that this isn't a circus at all. It's a showcase for skills in dance and magic, rather than the usual ones you expect in a circus. With only six performers it's a small production, which suits the venue well – the Studio only seats about two hundred people. For my money it's the aerial displays which are outstanding as well as the magical tricks – features which are missing from *Circus Romano*. An interesting feature of the show is that the performers are so young – the youngest is only fourteen. But it's still well worth seeing: a good one for <u>the whole family</u>.   *Q17*   *Q18*

And finally, as it's summer, you may wish to see some of the Festival performances that are being presented outdoors. Like the famous *Mekong Water Puppet Troupe*, performing in <u>the City Gardens</u> this week. Now, water puppetry is amazing! It's large puppets on long sticks, controlled by puppeteers standing waist deep in the lake. The puppets do comedy routines and there is some terrific formation dancing. This is a fantastic show and the best moment comes at the end – seeing the puppeteers. When the troupe walks up out of the water, you get this amazing feeling. It's really hard to believe that what you've been watching is lifeless wood and cloth. As an adult, I had a great time, but I did note that other older people in the audience weren't quite as taken with it as I was. It's a must for <u>young children</u> though, and that's the audience it's really aimed at.   *Q19*   *Q20*

Well, that's all I've time for today, but I'll be back next week with more news of what's worth seeing and what it's best to miss.

SECTION 3

OFFICER: Hello. Er, I'm Dawn Matthews.

STUDENT: Yes, hello. I've been referred to you because I'm enquiring about the refresher courses that you run. I'd like to find out a bit more about them.

OFFICER: OK. Well, we run quite a few different short courses for students who are either <u>returning to study</u> or studying part-time. Um, tell me about your situation.   *Q21*

STUDENT: Well, I think that I really need some help in preparing for the coming semester, especially to build up my confidence a bit and help me study effectively because, you see, I've been out in the work-force for nearly twelve years now, so it really is a long time since I was last a student.

OFFICER: Yes, it can seem like a long time, can't it? Um, well, let me start by telling you what courses we have that might suit you. Are you an undergraduate or a postgraduate? Arts or Sciences?

STUDENT: Undergraduate, and I'm in the Business faculty.

OFFICER: Right then. First of all, there's our intensive 'Study for Success' seminar on <u>the first and second</u> of February. It's aimed at students like you who are   *Q22* uncertain about what to expect at college, and looks at a fairly wide range of approaches to university learning, to motivate you to begin your study and build on your own learning strategies.

STUDENT: Mm, that sounds good. What are some of the strategies that are presented?

OFFICER: Well, we try to cover all aspects of study. Some of the strategies in writing, for example, would be improving your planning for writing, organising your thinking and building some techniques to help you <u>write more clearly</u>. With   *Q23* reading, there'll be sessions aimed at getting into the habit of <u>analysing</u>   *Q24* <u>material</u> as you read it, and tips to help you record and remember what you have read. It really is very important to begin reading confidently right from the beginning.

STUDENT: Mm.

OFFICER: There's also advice on how to get the most from your lectures and practice in giving confident presentations, as well as how to prepare for exams.

STUDENT: What about the motivational side of things?

OFFICER: Ah. Well, there's a range of motivational exercises that we do to help the students feel <u>positive and enthusiastic about their study</u>. The process of   *Q25* learning and exploring a subject can lead to a whole new way of looking at the world, and the study skills and techniques that you build up can be applied in all sorts of different ways.

STUDENT: Actually, I . . . I'm very excited about the whole thing of taking up studying again but, you know, I'm a little nervous about whether I'll manage to get everything done. I suppose it's the same for all mature students?

OFFICER: Of course it is. Two of the key components of the course are <u>time management</u>   *Q26* and overcoming procrastination. People discover that, once they learn to plan their days, all the work can be accomplished and there'll still be time for leisure.

STUDENT: Is there an enrolment fee?

OFFICER: Well, er, oh, just a minute, let's see . . . Ah, the cost is thirty pounds, which includes all course materials and morning tea. You have to arrange your own lunch.

STUDENT: That wouldn't be a problem. I already make sandwiches for my three kids and my wife and myself every day. I won't have to change my routine.

OFFICER: No. Now, I need to tell you that this is a very popular course and it's essential that you book well ahead of time. In fact, the Course Convenor tells me that there are only five places left. *Q27*

STUDENT: What other course might be good for me?

OFFICER: There is one other that you could benefit from. It's simply called 'Learning Skills for University Study' and is on three consecutive mornings starting on a Monday, from nine to twelve, and costs twenty-five pounds. This is aimed at upgrading the study skills most school-leavers have and help them cope with the increased demands of university study. It focuses mainly on making students more responsible for their own success. *Q28*

STUDENT: What sort of things are covered in this course?

OFFICER: Well, basically it's more advanced thinking, note-taking, reading and writing strategies, but also some input about stress management. *Q29*

STUDENT: I think I'd be better off starting from the basics and looking at all the strategies, don't you? *Q30*

OFFICER: Yes, from what you've told me, I think that's more in line with your situation.

STUDENT: Alright then, um, can I book a place on the 'Study for Success' seminar course now?

OFFICER: Yes. Let me just get out a registration form and take down your details.

SECTION 4

We're very grateful that the Committee has agreed that a representative for the Students' Union can present students' suggestions about the design for the proposed new Union building. We appreciate that some of our ideas may not be feasible in the circumstances, but we do feel that it is important that the ultimate beneficiaries of the facilities should have some say in its design.

If I could start by briefly explaining what steps were taken to find out student opinion and how we have arrived at conclusions. Firstly, a meeting was held in the current Union for our SU Committee to explain the options. Then we invited all students to submit written suggestions for the design, placing cards in a suggestion box. These suggestions then provided the basis for the design of a questionnaire, which was completed by approximately two thousand of the College students over a period of three weeks. Finally, the SU Committee collated the results and drew up a report. If I can just hand around a copy of that report. This presentation is essentially a summary and discussion of the key points of this report. *Q31, Q32*

So, in broad terms, the consensus was as follows. Firstly, regarding the crucial matter of the site, we presented the three options that you have proposed. One: in the city centre, near

the Faculty of <u>Education;</u> two: on the outskirts of the city, near the park, and three: out of   *Q33*
town, near the <u>halls of residence</u>. We asked students to cite reasons for and against these   *Q34*
sites and, and there was remarkable agreement on all three. Site One was unpopular
because of <u>traffic and parking problems</u>. Site Two had a number of supporters, mainly   *Q35*
because it was close to <u>most lecture rooms</u>. And Site Three, out of town, near the halls of   *Q36*
residence, was clearly the most popular because of access from living quarters. It was clear
that the Union was mainly to be used after lectures. It was also felt that the larger site
would allow <u>more room for a choice of facilities</u>.   *Q37*

Our second area of interest was obviously the facilities: there was minimal interest in
having a library on the premises, but one option seemed to be a reading room instead –
more useful. We would like the current table games room to be replaced with <u>a small gym</u>.   *Q38*
And, if possible, a small swimming pool – not, of course, Olympic-sized! There was a large
number of respondents in favour of <u>a travel agent's</u> and insurance centre. We also request
that there be the offices of the Student Counselling Centre, moving this from the Refectory.
There was, however, much disagreement about whether to build a drama theatre. Just over
forty per cent of the respondents were in favour, but a largish minority were strongly
against it, claiming that it is <u>elitist and a waste of funds</u>. Essentially the jury is out on that.   *Q39*

Finally, given the number of unfortunate incidents in the current Union over the past few
months, a strong point was repeatedly made about security. The recommendations would be
at least <u>video surveillance</u> and security personnel who would <u>check Student Union cards on</u>   *Q40*
<u>request</u>. We doubt if it would be feasible to have a check at reception of all people coming
in.

Well, this is the summary of the views of the student population. As I say, fuller details
are given in our report but I'm happy to take any questions if you have them . . . *(fade out)*

TEST 4

SECTION 1

LISA: Hi Tony, thanks ever so much for coming. You know we've been asked to organise
      something for John's farewell?

TONY: Yeah, sure, it's about time we started working out details.

LISA: Exactly. We don't want to leave it so late that it's double the work.

TONY: Mmm, mm, right, do you want me to take notes?

LISA: That'd be great, thanks.

TONY: Right, first thing is, when is the best time to hold it?

LISA: Well, he leaves on the twenty-fourth of December.

TONY   So what about the <u>twenty-second</u>?   *Example*

LISA: Yeah, I think that's about right. We want it quite near the time, don't we?

TONY: Sure, and what about a venue? In college? A hotel?

LISA: I think a hotel will probably work out rather expensive, and I've been looking at
      the <u>College Dining Room</u>; that seems pretty reasonable.   *Q1*

TONY:	Fine, yeah, why not?	
LISA:	And then we ought to be thinking about invitations . . . who mustn't we forget to invite?	
TONY:	Well, obviously John and his wife.	
LISA:	Right.	
TONY:	And the Director.	
LISA:	Ah ha.	
TONY:	The office staff.	Q2
LISA:	Yep, and all the teachers and all the students.	Q3
TONY:	Anyone else?	
LISA:	Faculty Heads?	
TONY:	No, better draw the line, I don't think it's necessary.	
LISA:	Yeah, you're right.	
TONY:	I don't mind writing the invitations. When shall we get them out for?	
LISA:	Enough time but not too early. What about the fifteenth of December?	
TONY:	Well, there are exams on the sixteenth – better avoid them.	
LISA:	Tenth?	Q4
TONY:	Yeah, that should do it.	

- -

LISA:	So what does that leave? Oh yes, a present.	
TONY:	Would you mind doing that?	
LISA:	No, not at all; we usually go round with an envelope during coffee break, don't we?	Q5
TONY:	Yeah, coffee break's always the best time, 'cos people have got their money handy.	
LISA:	Yeah, exactly. Do we suggest an amount? Or does it seem a bit unfair?	
TONY:	No, I think people welcome it. We suggested six dollars last time, is that OK?	Q6
LISA:	Yeah, plenty I would have thought, which should leave us with about ninety dollars.	
TONY:	Have you any ideas for presents?	
LISA:	Well, I've been having a little think. I thought, you know, he loves music.	
TONY:	Yeah, and books.	
LISA:	So, I thought I'd check on prices for, well, perhaps CD players.	
TONY:	Yeah, that's a good idea, and also I thought maybe, you know, a set of dictionaries. I heard him say he needed a good one.	Q7
LISA:	The other thing he was saying last week was that his computer printer had broken.	
TONY:	Umm. No, I'd be really frightened about getting the wrong type.	
LISA:	OK, yeah.	
TONY:	The other thing is something for the home – Jill suggested a coffee maker.	
LISA:	Oh yeah. I'll certainly find out what they cost. OK, have you got all that down?	
TONY:	Yes.	
LISA:	Now we need to think a little more about the money. I know we've got a set amount from the Social Fund.	
TONY:	Right, what does that cover?	
LISA:	It's meant to cover the cost of the room.	

TONY:	Yeah.	
LISA:	And a certain amount for food.	
TONY:	And also drinks?	
LISA:	Oh yeah, certainly.	
TONY:	But will it be enough?	
LISA:	What we've done in the past is to ask guests to bring some snacks.	
TONY:	Right.	
LISA:	We don't ask them to bring more drinks because we figure that's . . . that should come from the Social Fund.	
TONY:	OK. Anything else for the guests to bring?	
LISA:	Well, <u>some music</u>, because there'll be a tape deck there in the room, and we can have some dancing later on.	*Q8*
TONY:	Anything else?	
LISA:	Well, it's just a thought, but a couple of years ago we had a really good party where we set up, you know, some simple games.	
TONY:	Yeah, great. Wasn't it based on photos from the students and teachers?	
LISA:	That's right.	
TONY:	So we should ask the guests to bring <u>photos</u>. OK. I'll put it on the invitations.	*Q9*
LISA:	Now the last thing is, who shall we ask to do the <u>speech</u>?	*Q10*
TONY:	Don't you think it might be nice to have one of the students?	
LISA:	Well then, the Student Leader?	
TONY:	Yeah, much better than the Director giving speeches again.	
LISA:	OK then, I'll ask her. Lovely! So, is that all?	
TONY:	Looks like it.	
LISA:	Great. Thanks ever so much . . . *(fade out)*	

SECTION 2

SPEAKER 1:	Thank you for calling the free Travelite Travel Agency Information Line. You will not be charged for this call.	
	In order to deal with all calls effectively, we offer you a number of options. Please listen carefully and press your required number at the appropriate time, or dial a new number.	
	If you want to hear about special offers, please press one. If you want to hear our latest price lists, please press <u>two</u>. If you want to make a complaint, please press three. If you want information about our new walking holidays, please press four now.	*Q11*
SPEAKER 2:	Thank you for calling our Travelite Walking Holidays Line. We have been offering a wide variety of walking holidays to suit all tastes for just three years, but already we have won two awards for excellence in this field. We offer guided walking tours to suit the discerning traveller in twelve different centres throughout the whole of <u>Western Europe</u>. We are planning to open our first centre outside this area in the coming year, so watch out for developments.	*Q12*

But the pride of Travelite is the level of guidance and support we offer on our walks. All are planned in detail by our highly trained guides, who all work in a variety of different Travelite locations, so we can guarantee standards. Each day we offer three separate walks <u>catering for all skills and fitness levels</u>.   *Q13*

We also pride ourselves on our friendly service, particularly important for the increasing numbers of people who choose to holiday alone. Unlike almost all travel operators who happily charge large supplements for single rooms, we guarantee that <u>no single client will pay more</u>, even when only double rooms are available for them. And the day doesn't end with the return to base . . . after our dinner at communal tables designed to make all our guests feel part of a family atmosphere . . . entertainment is laid on <u>nearly every night</u> with tour leaders on hand to organise lectures, games, quizzes and respond to any special requests from guests.   *Q14* / *Q15*

The following is a summary of costs and special inclusive offers on holidays for the coming summer. We have three lengths of holiday: three-day, seven-day and fourteen-day. The three-day holiday costs <u>one hundred and eighty</u> dollars for all accommodation, food and walking, and for the first time this year we are including in that price . . . the cost of picking you up from the <u>nearest station</u>. The seven-day holiday costs three hundred and fifty dollars per person and, as well as including the offers of the three-day holiday, also includes a magnificent book giving the <u>local history</u>. On top of that, we are able to include free maps . . . for you to better enjoy the walking and even plan in advance, if you wish.   *Q16* / *Q17* / *Q18*

For the fourteen-day holiday, our special price is <u>six hundred and ninety</u> dollars per person and that includes all the offers for the three- and seven-day holidays plus . . . membership of a <u>local walking club</u> . . . so you can better enjoy the full flavour of the local life.   *Q19* / *Q20*

For further information, please contact your local travel agent. Thank for you calling the Travelite Travel Agency Information Line . . . *(fade out)*

SECTION 3

MIKE: Hi Sue.

SUE: Hi Mike, so what happened to you last week?

MIKE: Oh, I was sick with the flu. What's this I hear about a big assignment we've got to do?

SUE: Well, basically, we've got to find two science experiments to do with a group of eight-year-old children at the local primary school, and we've got to complete it by the end of the week.

MIKE: Oh, that sounds like hard work. Where are we supposed to get the ideas for these experiments from?

SUE: Well, I managed to get hold of two books from the library.

MIKE:	Oh, well done!
SUE:	How about if we take a look at the experiments in this book first and see if anything looks suitable? I can make notes as we go, about equipment and the purpose of the experiments.
MIKE:	OK, let's see, um, the first experiment is called 'Make your own hovercraft', which sounds very ambitious! Mind you, you only need <u>twenty balloons</u> and a table – you don't need any special engines or anything like that!

Q21 appears to the right of the balloons line.

SUE:	What do you do with it all?
MIKE:	Er, you blow up the balloons and you balance the table on them, upside down of course, and the kids get to ride around on it. You know, the other kids sort of push them around the room. The main purpose is to show how hovercrafts work, and how things hover around on just a cushion of air.
SUE:	OK, that doesn't sound too bad.
MIKE:	OK, ready for number two?
SUE:	Hmm, hmm.
MIKE:	Now this one is called 'Unusual Measures of Lengths', and you basically use lots of paperclips. The kids go around the class measuring things – you know, how long the desk is, and that sort of thing, um, and then they all compare their answers. Er, and, basically, because not all paperclips are the same lengths, they should come up with some strange answers. It's supposed to demonstrate the importance of having fixed <u>units of measurement</u>. *Q22*
SUE:	Hmm, yes, that's not bad.
MIKE:	OK, now for number three you need <u>rock salt</u> or copper sulphate. *Q23*
SUE:	Oh, I'm not sure about that!
MIKE:	Well, just put down the rock salt then, um, apart from that you only need a jar of water. Um, and basically you dissolve lots of salt into the water and watch the crystals form, so it basically teaches the kids about growing <u>crystals</u>. *Q24*
SUE:	I suppose it would be nice to grow something. Hmm, let's move on and have a look at number four.
MIKE:	OK, this one is called 'Spinning colour wheel'. It looks like you get some cardboard and draw a circle on it, divide it into six equal segments and colour each one in using different colours, then you thread a <u>piece of string</u> through the middle. *Q25*
SUE:	So we'd need some string as well.
MIKE:	Yes, sorry . . . um . . . and you spin the wheel around and if you can get it spinning fast enough, hopefully the colours all merge and show up as white.
SUE:	Oh, I didn't know that. What's the principle behind it?
MIKE:	Well it's pretty elementary physics, really. It teaches them about how <u>white light or ordinary light</u> is made up. *Q26*
SUE:	Hmm, well that doesn't sound too bad. Now there's only one more left in this book isn't there? What does that one say?
MIKE:	Um, well it's another one where they'd get to make something.
SUE:	Sounds very interesting.
MIKE:	You need quite a lot of equipment actually – a hand drill, an old record, a pin or needle, some paper and a bolt.

SUE:	Hmm, go on, what do they have to do?	
MIKE:	Well, they basically make a record player. The main idea is to teach them about recording sound, but hopefully they'd also see that you need motion and an amplifier to make the sound heard.	
SUE:	OK, well it does sound interesting. Shall we go through all of those again and decide if any of them are going to be suitable?	

MIKE:	Right, number one. I thought this one sounded nice: there'd be lots of activity and it doesn't need too much in the way of equipment.	
SUE:	Yes, that's true, but don't you think it's <u>a bit risky</u> to get a group of eight-year-olds pushing each other around a classroom like that? Someone could get hurt. No, I don't like the sound of that one at all!	*Q27*
MIKE:	Maybe you're right.	
SUE:	What about number two, with the paperclips? It sounds tame enough.	
MIKE:	Yes, a bit too tame if you ask me. I think it needs to be something <u>a bit more active and interesting</u> than that, don't you?	*Q28*
SUE:	Yes, I suppose you're right. We won't get a very good mark if the children don't actually enjoy the experiments, and I suppose we could turn them off science for good! Well, what about the next one, number three?	
MIKE:	Now, I quite like the idea of this one.	
SUE:	Yes, so do I, but I seem to remember when we did it at high school we <u>had to wait up to a fortnight</u> before we saw any halfway decent results.	*Q29*
MIKE:	Oh, yes well, that won't be any good then. We'll only see the kids for one or two hours at the most.	
SUE:	Yes, and we have to do the experiments and write up our results within a week, so that one won't do at all.	
MIKE:	OK, well, what did you think of number four?	
SUE:	I like the idea of it, but do you think it will be a bit elementary for them?	
MIKE:	Well they are only eight you know!	
SUE:	I know, but you know what I mean. Don't you think the activity itself is a bit babyish?	
MIKE:	Hmm, maybe you're right.	
SUE:	They might have fun but, I mean, cutting out a circle and colouring it in?	
MIKE:	OK, well, what about number five?	
SUE:	I thought this one sounded a bit too good to be true – great equipment!	
MIKE:	Yeah.	
SUE:	But don't you think it's <u>a bit ambitious</u> for this age group? I mean, I don't want to start off something and then have to abandon it if they just can't cope with it. I could see us ending up doing just about all of the work for them.	*Q30*
MIKE:	I guess you're right. Oh well, maybe we could store that idea away for later.	
SUE:	Yep, let's hope this second book has something better!	

SECTION 4

Today we're going to look at one of my favourite fish – the shark. As you know, sharks have a reputation for being very dangerous creatures capable of injuring or killing humans, and I'd like to talk about sharks in Australia.

    Sharks are rather large fish, often growing to over ten metres and the longest sharks caught in Australia have reached sixteen metres. Sharks vary in weight with size and breed, of course, but the heaviest shark caught in Australia was a White Pointer – that weighed <u>seven hundred and ninety-five</u> kilograms – quite a size! Sharks have a different structure to   *Q31* most fish: instead of a skeleton made of bone, they have a tough elastic skeleton of cartilage. Unlike bone, this firm, pliable material is rather like your nose, and allows the shark to bend easily as it swims. The shark's skin isn't covered with scales, like other fish: instead the skin's covered with barbs, giving it a rough texture like sandpaper. As you know, sharks are very quick swimmers. This is made possible by their fins, one set at the side and another set underneath the body, and the <u>tail</u> also helps the shark move forward quickly.   *Q32*

    Unlike other fish, sharks have to keep swimming if they want to stay at a particular depth, and they rarely swim at the surface. Mostly, they swim at the bottom of the ocean, scavenging and picking up food that's lying on the ocean <u>floor</u>. While most other animals,   *Q33* including fish, hunt their prey by means of their eyesight, sharks hunt essentially by smell. They have a very acute <u>sense of smell</u> – and can sense the presence of food long before they   *Q34* can see it.

    In Australia, where people spend a lot of time at the beach, the government has realised that it must prevent sharks from swimming near its beaches. As a result, they've introduced a beach-netting program. Beach-netting, or meshing, involves <u>setting large nets parallel to</u>   *Q35* <u>the shore</u>; this means that the nets on New South Wales beaches are set on one day, and then lifted and taken out to sea on the next day. When shark-netting first began in 1939, only the Sydney metropolitan beaches were meshed – these beaches were chosen because beaches near the city are usually the most crowded with swimmers. Ten years later, in 1949, systematic meshing was extended to include the beaches to the south of Sydney. As a result of the general success of the program in Sydney, shark-meshing was introduced to the state of Queensland around 1970. The New Zealand authorities also looked at it, but considered meshing uneconomical – as did Tahiti in the Pacific. At around the same time, <u>South Africa</u>   *Q36* introduced meshing to some of its most popular swimming beaches.

    When meshing began, approximately fifteen hundred sharks were caught in the first year. However, this declined in the years that followed, and since that time, the average annual catch has been only about <u>a hundred and fifty</u> a year. The majority of sharks are caught   *Q37* <u>during the warmest months, from November to February</u>, when sharks are most active and   *Q38* when both the air and the ocean are at their maximum temperature.

    Despite quite large catches, some people believe that shark meshing is not the best way to catch sharks. It's not that they think sharks are afraid of nets, or because they eat holes in them, because neither of these is true. But meshing does appear to be less effective than some other methods, especially when there are big seas with <u>high rolling waves and strong</u>   *Q39* <u>currents</u> and anything that lets <u>the sand move</u> – the sand that's holding the nets down.   *Q40* When this moves the nets will also become less effective.

Answer key

TEST 1

LISTENING

Each question correctly answered scores 1 mark. **CORRECT SPELLING IS NEEDED IN ALL ANSWERS.**

Section 1, Questions 1–10

1 shopping / variety of shopping
2 guided tours
3 more than 12 / over 12
4 notice board
5 13th February
6 Tower of London
7 Bristol
8 American Museum
9 student newspaper
10 Yentob

Section 2, Questions 11–20

11 **IN EITHER ORDER, BOTH REQUIRED FOR ONE MARK**
   coal
   firewood
12 local craftsmen
13 160
14 Woodside
15 Ticket Office
16 Gift Shop
17 (main) Workshop
18 Showroom
19 Café
20 cottages

Section 3, Questions 21–30

21 A
22 C
23 E
24 B
25 G
26 F
27 C
28 D
29 A
30 B

Section 4, Questions 31–40

31 cities / environment
32 windy
33 humid
34 shady / shaded
35 dangerous
36 leaves
37 ground
38 considerably reduce / decrease / filter
39 low
40 space / room

If you score . . .

0–14	15–30	31–40
you are highly unlikely to get an acceptable score under examination conditions and we recommend that you spend a lot of time improving your English before you take IELTS.	you may get an acceptable score under examination conditions but we recommend that you think about having more practice or lessons before you take IELTS.	you are likely to get an acceptable score under examination conditions but remember that different institutions will find different scores acceptable.

152

ACADEMIC READING

Each question correctly answered scores 1 mark. **CORRECT SPELLING IS NEEDED IN ALL ANSWERS.**

Reading Passage 1, Questions 1–14

1   FALSE
2   FALSE
3   TRUE
4   TRUE
5   FALSE
6   NOT GIVEN
7   TRUE
8   NOT GIVEN
9   M
10 E
11 G
12 P
13 J
14 B

Reading Passage 2, Questions 15–26

15 taste buds
16 baleen / the baleen whales
17 *IN EITHER ORDER, BOTH REQUIRED FOR ONE MARK*
    forward
    downward
18 freshwater dolphin(s) / the freshwater dolphin(s)
19 water / the water

20 lower frequencies / the lower frequencies
21 *IN EITHER ORDER, BOTH REQUIRED FOR ONE MARK*
    bowhead
    humpback
22 touch / sense of touch
23 freshwater dolphin(s) / the freshwater dolphin(s)
24 airborne flying fish
25 clear water(s) / clear open water(s)
26 acoustic sense / the acoustic sense

Reading Passage 3, Questions 27–40

27 C
28 C
29 A
30 E
31 C
32 A
33 pairs
34 shapes
35 sighted
36 sighted
37 deep
38 blind
39 similar
40 B

If you score . . .

0–12	13–26	27–40
you are highly unlikely to get an acceptable score under examination conditions and we recommend that you spend a lot of time improving your English before you take IELTS.	you may get an acceptable score under examination conditions but we recommend that you think about having more practice or lessons before you take IELTS.	you are likely to get an acceptable score under examination conditions but remember that different institutions will find different scores acceptable.

TEST 2

LISTENING

Each question correctly answered scores 1 mark. **CORRECT SPELLING IS NEEDED IN ALL ANSWERS.**

Section 1, Questions 1–10

1	C
2	C
3	B
4	B
5	A
6	Cathedral
7	Markets
8	Gardens
9	Art Gallery
10	climb the tower / see the view

Section 2, Questions 11–20

11	C
12	B
13	A
14	C
15	B
16	C
17	A
18	B
19	B
20	A

Section 3, Questions 21–30

21	collecting data / gathering data / data collection
22	1,500
23	5
24	3,000–4,000
25 & 26	**IN EITHER ORDER**
	B
	C
27	Mehta
28	Survey Research
29	London University / London University Press
30	1988

Section 4, Questions 31–40

31	C
32	A
33	mass media / media
34	academic circles / academics / researchers
35	specialist knowledge / specialised knowledge
36	unaware
37	individual customers / individual consumers / individuals
38	illegal profit / illegal profits
39 & 40	**IN EITHER ORDER**
	D
	E

If you score . . .

0–13	14–28	29–40
you are highly unlikely to get an acceptable score under examination conditions and we recommend that you spend a lot of time improving your English before you take IELTS.	you may get an acceptable score under examination conditions but we recommend that you think about having more practice or lessons before you take IELTS.	you are likely to get an acceptable score under examination conditions but remember that different institutions will find different scores acceptable.

ACADEMIC READING

Each question correctly answered scores 1 mark. **CORRECT SPELLING IS NEEDED IN ALL ANSWERS.**

Reading Passage 1, Questions 1–13

1	isolation
2	economic globalisation / globalization / socio-economic pressures
3	cultural identity
4	traditional skill
5	E
6	B
7	D
8	C
9	B
10	NO
11	YES
12	NOT GIVEN
13	YES

Reading Passage 2, Questions 14–26

14	C
15	B
16	YES
17	NO
18	YES
19	YES
20	YES
21	NOT GIVEN
22	NO
23	YES
24	emotional / emotional problems
25	headache / headaches
26	general ill health

Reading Passage 3, Questions 27–40

27	H
28	F
29	A
30	H
31	I
32	B
33–35	*IN ANY ORDER*
	A
	C
	F
36	B
37	G
38	E
39	D
40	A

If you score . . .

0–13	14–27	28–40
you are highly unlikely to get an acceptable score under examination conditions and we recommend that you spend a lot of time improving your English before you take IELTS.	you may get an acceptable score under examination conditions but we recommend that you think about having more practice or lessons before you take IELTS.	you are likely to get an acceptable score under examination conditions but remember that different institutions will find different scores acceptable.

TEST 3

LISTENING

Each question correctly answered scores 1 mark. **CORRECT SPELLING IS NEEDED IN ALL ANSWERS.**

Section 1, Questions 1–10

1	1½ years
2	Forest / Forrest
3	Academic
4	Thursday
5	B
6	B
7	A
8	deposit
9	monthly
10	telephone / phone

Section 2, Questions 11–20

11	C
12	A
13	C
14	B
15	lighting / lights / light
16	adult / adults
17	(at) Studio Theatre / (the) Studio Theatre / (at) Studio Theater / (the) Studio Theater
18	the whole family / all the family / families
19	(in) City Gardens / the City Gardens / outdoors
20	young children / younger children / children

Section 3, Questions 21–30

21	A
22	B
23	C
24	A
25	B
26	A
27	C
28	B
29	B
30	B

Section 4, Questions 31–40

31	questionnaire
32	approximately 2,000 / about 2,000
33	Education
34	halls of residence / living quarters
35	*IN EITHER ORDER, BOTH REQUIRED FOR ONE MARK* traffic / parking
36	(most) lecture rooms / lecture halls / lecture theatres / lecture theaters
37	(choice of) facilities / (room for) facilities
38	*IN EITHER ORDER, BOTH REQUIRED FOR ONE MARK* D / F
39	B
40	*IN EITHER ORDER, BOTH REQUIRED FOR ONE MARK* A / C

If you score . . .

0–12	13–27	28–40
you are highly unlikely to get an acceptable score under examination conditions and we recommend that you spend a lot of time improving your English before you take IELTS.	you may get an acceptable score under examination conditions but we recommend that you think about having more practice or lessons before you take IELTS.	you are likely to get an acceptable score under examination conditions but remember that different institutions will find different scores acceptable.

ACADEMIC READING

Each question correctly answered scores 1 mark. **CORRECT SPELLING IS NEEDED IN ALL ANSWERS.**

Reading Passage 1, Questions 1–13

1   A
2   D
3   C
4   C
5   *IN EITHER ORDER, BOTH REQUIRED FOR ONE MARK*
    Sudan
    India
6   bicycles
7   Shoe Shine / Shoe Shine Collective
8   life skills
9   NO
10 NOT GIVEN
11 NO
12 YES
13 A

Reading Passage 2, Questions 14–26

14 iii
15 i
16 iv
17 vi
18 plates / the plates / the tectonic plates
19 magma
20 ring of fire
21 600 / 600 years / for 600 years
22 water / the water / oceans / the oceans
23 lava / magma / molten rock
24 India / western India
25 explodes
26 gases / the gases / trapped gases

Reading Passage 3, Questions 27–40

27 D
28 E
29 C
30 D
31 F
32 (the) linguist (acts) / (the) linguists (act)
33 foreign languages
34 quality / the quality / the poor quality
35 non-verbal behaviour / non-verbal behavior / facial expression / facial expressions
36 camera / video camera / recording / video recording
37 frequency of usage / usage frequency
38 particular linguistic feature
39 size
40 intuitions

If you score . . .

0–12	13–27	28–40
you are highly unlikely to get an acceptable score under examination conditions and we recommend that you spend a lot of time improving your English before you take IELTS.	you may get an acceptable score under examination conditions but we recommend that you think about having more practice or lessons before you take IELTS.	you are likely to get an acceptable score under examination conditions but remember that different institutions will find different scores acceptable.

TEST 4

LISTENING

Each question correctly answered scores 1 mark. **CORRECT SPELLING IS NEEDED IN ALL ANSWERS.**

Section 1, Questions 1–10

1 College Dining Room
2 & 3 *IN EITHER ORDER*
office staff
students
4 10th December
5 coffee break / coffee breaks
6 6
7 set of dictionaries / dictionaries / a good dictionary
8 & 9 *IN EITHER ORDER*
(some) music / (some) music tapes / (some) tapes
photos / photographs
10 speech

Section 2, Questions 11–20

11 B
12 A
13 A
14 A
15 B
16 180
17 nearest station
18 local history
19 690
20 walking club / local walking club

Section 3, Questions 21–30

21 20 balloons
22 units of measurement / measurements / measurement units
23 rock salt / salt
24 crystals
25 string / piece of string
26 (ordinary) (white) light
27 H
28 B
29 E
30 C

Section 4, Questions 31–40

31 795
32 tail
33 floor / bed / bottom
34 sense of smell
35 A
36 A
37 B
38 B
39 & 40 *IN EITHER ORDER*
B
E

If you score . . .

0–12	13–27	28–40
you are highly unlikely to get an acceptable score under examination conditions and we recommend that you spend a lot of time improving your English before you take IELTS.	you may get an acceptable score under examination conditions but we recommend that you think about having more practice or lessons before you take IELTS.	you are likely to get an acceptable score under examination conditions but remember that different institutions will find different scores acceptable.

ACADEMIC READING

Each question correctly answered scores 1 mark. **CORRECT SPELLING IS NEEDED IN ALL ANSWERS.**

Reading Passage 1, Questions 1–13

1	TRUE
2	NOT GIVEN
3	FALSE
4	FALSE
5	NOT GIVEN
6	TRUE
7	genetics
8	power
9	injuries
10	training
11	A
12	D
13	B

Reading Passage 2, Questions 14–27

14	YES
15	NOT GIVEN
16	NO
17	YES
18	NOT GIVEN
19	NO
20 & 21	***IN EITHER ORDER***
	D
	E

22 & 23	***IN EITHER ORDER***
	C
	D
24	oral histories
25 & 26	***IN EITHER ORDER***
	humanistic study
	historical discipline
27	scientist

Reading Passage 3, Questions 28–40

28	iv
29	i
30	iii
31	v
32	B
33	B
34	A
35	B
36	NO
37	YES
38	YES
39	NOT GIVEN
40	NOT GIVEN

If you score . . .

0–12	13–28	29–40
you are highly unlikely to get an acceptable score under examination conditions and we recommend that you spend a lot of time improving your English before you take IELTS.	you may get an acceptable score under examination conditions but we recommend that you think about having more practice or lessons before you take IELTS.	you are likely to get an acceptable score under examination conditions but remember that different institutions will find different scores acceptable.

GENERAL TRAINING TEST A

READING

Each question correctly answered scores 1 mark. **CORRECT SPELLING IS NEEDED IN ALL ANSWERS.**

Section 1, Questions 1–14

1	B
2	A
3	E
4	C
5	A
6	C
7	D
8	B
9	B
10	E
11	D
12	A
13	B
14	D

Section 2, Questions 15–27

15	TRUE
16	FALSE
17	NOT GIVEN
18	TRUE
19	NOT GIVEN
20	NOT GIVEN
21	F
22	A
23	G
24	B
25	E
26	H
27	C

Section 3, Questions 28–40

28–30	*IN ANY ORDER*
	A
	D
	F
31	*IN EITHER ORDER, BOTH REQUIRED FOR ONE MARK*
	cartoons
	serials
32	(slapstick) comedy / slapstick
33	(the) avant(-)garde (film(s))
34	A
35	C
36	H
37	C
38	A
39	F
40	D

If you score . . .

0–16	17–30	31–40
you are highly unlikely to get an acceptable score under examination conditions and we recommend that you spend a lot of time improving your English before you take IELTS.	you may get an acceptable score under examination conditions but we recommend that you think about having more practice or lessons before you take IELTS.	you are likely to get an acceptable score under examination conditions but remember that different institutions will find different scores acceptable.

GENERAL TRAINING TEST B

READING

Each question correctly answered scores 1 mark. **CORRECT SPELLING IS NEEDED IN ALL ANSWERS.**

Section 1, Questions 1–14

1	TRUE
2	FALSE
3	TRUE
4	TRUE
5	FALSE
6	FALSE
7	FALSE
8	B
9	D
10	K
11	L
12	G
13	J
14	A

Section 2, Questions 15–27

15	B
16	H
17	K
18	E
19	D
20	I
21	F
22	TRUE
23	FALSE
24	NOT GIVEN
25	NOT GIVEN
26	FALSE
27	FALSE

Section 3, Questions 28–40

28	vi
29	iv
30	x
31	viii
32	vii
33	ii
34	v
35, 36 & 37	*IN ANY ORDER*
	round
	sickle
	waggle
38	the feeding dish
39	the food (source)
40	the sun

If you score . . .

0–14	15–30	31–40
you are highly unlikely to get an acceptable score under examination conditions and we recommend that you spend a lot of time improving your English before you take IELTS.	you may get an acceptable score under examination conditions but we recommend that you think about having more practice or lessons before you take IELTS.	you are likely to get an acceptable score under examination conditions but remember that different institutions will find different scores acceptable.

Model and sample answers for Writing tasks

TEST 1, WRITING TASK 1

MODEL ANSWER

This model has been prepared by an examiner as an example of a very good answer. However, please note that this is just one example out of many possible approaches.

The table gives a breakdown of the different types of family who were living in poverty in Australia in 1999.

On average, 11% of all households, comprising almost two million people, were in this position. However, those consisting of only one parent or a single adult had almost double this proportion of poor people, with 21% and 19% respectively.

Couples generally tended to be better off, with lower poverty levels for couples without children (7%) than those with children (12%). It is noticeable that for both types of household with children, a higher than average proportion were living in poverty at this time.

Older people were generally less likely to be poor, though once again the trend favoured elderly couples (only 4%) rather than single elderly people (6%).

Overall the table suggests that households of single adults and those with children were more likely to be living in poverty than those consisting of couples.

TEST 1, WRITING TASK 2

SAMPLE ANSWER

This is an answer written by a candidate who achieved a Band 4 score. Here is the examiner's comment:

> This answer describes some relevant advantages and disadvantages of books, TV and films, although these are sometimes unclear or not sufficiently developed. The script loses marks, however, because it doesn't answer the question about 'which medium is most effective' and also because it is under the minimum length (only 230 words).
>
> The writer has tried to organise ideas and uses paragraphing to structure the response. However, the message is confused at times and the answer is incomplete. Some ideas are linked appropriately, but there is a lot of repetition across sentences.
>
> The writer uses a limited range of language quite repetitively and there are only simple sentences. However, these are often quite accurate, although there are many examples of basic errors in grammar and punctuation.

In our daily life, we always communicate information through the media, such as television, radio, film, These media have different advantages and disadvantages for us. Now, I am going to compare the advantages and disadvantages of books, television and film.

Books bring us different knowledge. It bases on what Book we read. A famous Chinese traditional verse which described books is a treasure. We can find a golden house in there. Moreover, when we want to read it, we can find it easily, such as bookstore, library. We can also learn a lot of words from books. And it can improve our reading and writing skills.

However, books always are not attractive for children or youngster. It is because books are quite boring. A lot of words and less pictures inside the books, compare to television, television has pictures and sound, We don't have to read a lot of words in television. But some artist in television programme or film, bring a bad image to us. Then some children or youngers will imitate their behaviour. Some film also bring a wrong message to us, For example, they are always smoking in films. It seems that smoking is good and smart. It caused many youngers imitate them smoking.

In conclusion, bookds, televison and film have many advantages and disadvantages. I cannot write all in here. And we have choose the media carefully.

Model and sample answers for Writing tasks

TEST 2, WRITING TASK 1

SAMPLE ANSWER

This is an answer written by a candidate who achieved a Band 6 score. Here is the examiner's comment:

> This answer focuses too closely on the details in the graph but fails to compare trends or general differences between figures for winter and summer. Some comparisons are made, but these are about details, and it is difficult to get a clear idea of the information from this description.
>
> Similarly, information in the pie chart is simply listed using the language from the chart and there is no attempt to relate this to information in the graph.
>
> The description is not well organised, although a range of linkers are used, and the use of paragraphs does not reflect the different sections of information covered.
>
> There is a suitable range of vocabulary for this task, although some words are misused and there are several spelling errors. The range and control of grammatical structures is the strong point of the main part of this response. There are examples of complex structures that are used with accuracy and some flexibility.

The use of electricity in England is indispensed with. Demand for electricity in England during typical days in winter and summer is illustrated in the graph. The use of electricity in an average English home is shown in the pie chart. From the graph, It is generally obvious that the demand is in its maximum around 2100, and in its minimum around 600, being almost constant between 1200 and 2100 in winter times. During summer times, on the other hand, the demand reaches its top point around 1300, and the bottom point around 900, being almost constant between 1550 and 2000.

In Winter times, the curve gradually increares to reach 40,000 units of electricity by 3 o'clock in the morning. This is followed by gradual decline to its lowest limite of 30,000 units at 9 o'clock. A gradual rise is obvious again to reach a stationary level between 3 o'clock and 9 o'clock of about 40,000 units again. Then, there is a sharp rise in the next hour to rech its maximum before collapsing again to a lower level by the end of the day.

In summer time, the curve gradually decrease to reach its lower limit around 9 o'clock of a bit more than 10,000 units. A gradual increase is noticed to reach its top of 20,000 after which a stationary phase is obvious between 3 o'clock and 10 o'clock at night of about 15,000 unites.

The pie chart, on the other hand, shows that 52.5% of the electricity is used for heating rooms and water. 17.5% is consumed for ovens, kettles and washing machines, 15% is used in lighting, TV and radio, and finally 15% is consumed in the sue of vacuum cleaners, food mixtures and electric tools.

TEST 2, WRITING TASK 2

MODEL ANSWER

This model has been prepared by an examiner as an example of a very good answer. However, please note that this is just one example out of many possible approaches.

Happiness is very difficult to define, because it means so many different things to different people. While some people link happiness to wealth and material success, others think it lies in emotions and loving personal relationships. Yet others think that spiritual paths, rather than either the material world or relationships with people, are the only way to true happiness.

Because people interpret happiness for themselves in so many different ways, it is difficult to give any definition that is true for everyone. However, if there are different kinds of happiness for different individuals then the first step in achieving it would be to have a degree of self-knowledge. A person needs to know who he or she is before being able to know what it is that makes him or her happy.

Of course, factors such as loving relationships, good health, the skills to earn a living and a peaceful environment all contribute to our happiness too. But this does not mean that people without these conditions cannot be happy.

Overall, I think an ability to keep clear perspectives in life is a more essential factor in achieving happiness. By that I mean an ability to have a clear sense of what is important in our lives (the welfare of our families, the quality of our relationships, making other people happy, etc.) and what is not (a problem at work, getting annoyed about trivial things, etc.).

Like self-awareness, this is also very difficult to achieve, but I think these are the two factors that may be the most important for achieving happiness.

TEST 3, WRITING TASK 1

MODEL ANSWER

This model has been prepared by an examiner as an example of a very good answer. However, please note that this is just one example out of many possible approaches.

> The chart gives information about post-school qualifications in terms of the different levels of further education reached by men and women in Australia in 1999.
>
> We can see immediately that there were substantial differences in the proportion of men and women at different levels. The biggest gender difference is at the lowest post-school level, where 90% of those who held a skilled vocational diploma were men, compared with only 10% of women. By contrast, more women held undergraduate diplomas (70%) and marginally more women reached degree level (55%).
>
> At the higher levels of education, men with postgraduate diplomas clearly outnumbered their female counterparts (70% and 30%, respectively), and also constituted 60% of Master's graduates.
>
> Thus we can see that more men than women hold qualifications at the lower and higher levels of education, while more women reach undergraduate diploma level than men. The gender difference is smallest at the level of Bachelor's degree, however.

TEST 3, WRITING TASK 2

SAMPLE ANSWER

This is an answer written by a candidate who achieved a Band 7 score. Here is the examiner's comment:

> This answer considers the main issues raised by the question and presents a definite opinion about the statement. However, the response tends to over-generalise and sometimes the examples used to support ideas seem rather confusing. Ideas are generally clearly organised, and paragraphing is clear but the argument is difficult to follow in places. A range of linking words and expressions is used, but there are occasional mistakes. The candidate uses an ambitious range of vocabulary and sentence patterns, but has some problems with word choice and collocations. There are very few spelling errors and only minor grammar mistakes, but there are many examples of expressions used inappropriately.

I agree with the statement that there should be no government restriction on creative artists who express themselves in the way they do and that they must be given freedom for the same. Expression has always been the keynote in a person's life. It is the result of mere expression of our thoughts that we are able to communicate. Restrictions on how we present our thoughts is senseless.

Creative artists play a major role in our society, be it the government, old people, the youth or the children. Their works enlighten our minds, no matter if is factual or entertainment based. It is diserving that after a days work when we want to take some time off for ourselves, we look out for some leisure. For instance: either pleasant music or a family movie which soothes the mind. Entertainment give us an overview of a new side of life which every individual respects. There is almost everything good in what is given to us through the media world which is made up of artists.

On the contrary sometimes these artists tend to be unscrupulous. They convert rumours into facts and present them before us. This might impair the reputation of some illustrious people in today's society. On such occasions, certain restrictions are understandable. Nevertheless we all do know what is right or wrong. Rules and regulations not always are the solution to how artists present their own ideas. Hence it is doltish to be impetuous and the government should enforce alternative ways to control the media.

Respect for ones ideas is not only hypothetical but must be practised. It is through respect that each one of us can be recognised as a unique person in the world. This can be achieved by looking at the bright side of what media i.e. the creative artists display for us. Not a day can go by when we dont look out for colourful dreams and a beautiful life which we can find either through music, poetry, films, pictures; everything that the creative artists offer us.

TEST 4, WRITING TASK 1

SAMPLE ANSWER

This is an answer written by a candidate who achieved a Band 5 score. Here is the examiner's comment:

> The response is under-length (138 words). The candidate reports the key information in the first graph i.e. that visits to and from the UK increased and that the increase in visits from the UK was more marked than that of visits to the country. In the bar chart the information is also reported accurately. However, the references to &dollar are confusing, suggesting that the candidate has not fully understood the information given, and there is little attempt to relate the two diagrams or to make comparisons across the information given.
>
> There is a brief introduction to the topic, with an attempt to paraphrase the rubric; the overall structure of the writing is clear, with some use of basic discourse markers. There is very little use of reference, however, resulting in a considerable amount of repetition of key vocabulary.
>
> There is a fairly narrow range of sentence types and errors occur in verb formation and in the use of tenses.

The graphs reveal an information about overseas residents travel to UK and UK residents travel to other countries, and where they visited more.

According to the chart of visits to and from UK, UK residents had visited abroad more than overseas residents visited UK. UK residents traveling were increased slightly till 1986, after that, there was a dramatic rise from $20 millions to $54 millions till 1999. In contrast, overseas residents were increased gradually in traveling to UK from $10 million to $28 millions between 1979 and 1999.

From the information shown, we can see that France was the most popular country visited by UK residents, accounting for $11 millions. And the others countries visited by UK residents were Turkey, Greece and USA, which were $3, $4 and $5 millions.

TEST 4, WRITING TASK 2

MODEL ANSWER

This model has been prepared by an examiner as an example of a very good answer. However, please note that this is just one example out of many possible approaches.

Poor student behaviour seems to be an increasingly widespread problem and I think that modern lifestyles are probably responsible for this.

In many countries, the birth rate is decreasing so that families are smaller with fewer children. These children are often spoilt, not in terms of love and attention because working parents do not have the time for this, but in more material ways. They are allowed to have whatever they want, regardless of price, and to behave as they please. This means that the children grow up without consideration for others and without any understanding of where their standard of living comes from.

When they get to school age they have not learnt any self control or discipline. They have less respect for their teachers and refuse to obey school rules in the way that their parents did.

Teachers continually complain about this problem and measures should be taken to combat the situation. But I think the solution to the problem lies with the families, who need to be more aware of the future consequences of spoiling their children. If they could raise them to be considerate of others and to be social, responsible individuals, the whole community would benefit.

Perhaps parenting classes are needed to help them to do this, and high quality nursery schools could be established that would support families more in terms of raising the next generation. The government should fund this kind of parental support, because this is no longer a problem for individual families, but for society as a whole.

TEST A, WRITING TASK 1 (GENERAL TRAINING)

SAMPLE ANSWER

This is an answer written by a candidate who achieved a Band 7 score. Here is the examiner's comment:

> This is a well-developed response to the task prompt. The letter has a clear purpose, it is written in an appropriate style and it gives all the information required by the bullet points. The situation is described in a relevant way and the letter communicates effectively and fluently.
>
> The information in the letter is organised, but there are no paragraphs so the reader has to work harder to follow the changes from one topic to the next and in some cases the links between sentences could be improved.
>
> A good range of vocabulary is used accurately, including idiomatic expressions. But some words are not well chosen so there are also awkward expressions that do not sound natural, and there are several examples of these.
>
> The writing includes a good range of grammatical structures which are usually used accurately. There are a few errors in grammar, and the first sentence lacks capital letters, which is a rather basic mistake.

Dear Sir or Madam,

my name is Liam Test, i'm the student that got hurt in the accident in front of your row of bean-tins in your supermarket. Let me give you some details about the accident first. I was just going around the corner from the vegetables to beans when a pregnant woman crashed into me with her shopping cart. It was impossible to see each other before the accident because this special corner is very dark and the lights didn't even work, probably because the eight bulbs were old and didn't serve anymore. Anyway, the floor was very slippery and wet because the rain was dripping through the non-waterproof ceiling, so I slipped, fell, and knocked myself out on the bean-tins. I lost consciousness. Your insurance payed for the accident but let me just give you some advice to prevent further accidents in your supermarket: make sure your ceiling is fixed and the floor is dry. You could also arrange your rows in a way that makes it possible for your customers to take care of each other. Always get the lights checked at leas once a week, and change damaged lightbulbs immediately. This would help making our supermarket a safer place.
Sincerely yours, . . .

TEST A, WRITING TASK 2 (GENERAL TRAINING)

SAMPLE ANSWER

This is an answer written by a candidate who achieved a Band 6 score. Here is the examiner's comment:

The writing focuses on the first question but does not address the second one directly. The candidate loses marks for this.

However, the writer's point of view is clear and there are some relevant ideas that are communicated effectively. Ideas are generally supported, and the argument is organised with some clear linking, although paragraphing is not always used appropriately.

A fairly wide range of language is attempted with mixed success. There are some good idiomatic expressions and some accurate complex sentences, but the writer misuses quite basic words and grammatical structures as well. The errors are quite frequent, but the writer's message can still be followed throughout the response.

In the past the people used to make clothes and doing repairs on things in the house more than nowadays. This is caused for many aspects that are present in our days like the quantity of other activities available to do, the differences in jobs and in lifestyle.

When in the past days the people finished their workday, it was still early and they had not too many other activities to do, so they spended their free time doing some of the repairs. While, in the other hand most of the women used to make clothes.

Nowadays is bigger the number of women that works, in addition to that, the work is normally longer and more stressing for everybody, so the people is getting used to live as fast as possible.

Another element that is pushing to this situation is that as the people is having less and less time for a hobby, any hobby will require more and more time. Because everything that you want to try to repair is more technical and complicated than before, and to do some repair the people almost have to be a qualified technician.

On top of all that the tradition is being lost because the people learn the traditions when they are young and from their parents, but nowadays the young people have too many distractions and hobbies like sports, going to shopping malls, video games, computers, cinema, amusement parks, e-mail and chat rooms, instead of spending their free time with their parents.

This situation is happening in the entire world, and it's caused in part by the globalisation and the advance of the technology in the home.

So the situation is that when the people need more knowledge to their hobbies, they have less time to acquire it because of their work. And that to transmit the traditions to other generations the adults need the young's people attention which they don't have because of new distractions the youngs have.

TEST B, WRITING TASK 1 (GENERAL TRAINING)

MODEL ANSWER

This model has been prepared by an examiner as an example of a very good answer. However, please note that this is just one example out of many possible approaches.

Dear Jan,

As you know, we'll be moving to a new house soon and there are a few things that I won't be able to take with me. The new house is a bit smaller so I have to sell some furniture and I was wondering if you might be interested?

In particular I want to sell my big dining table. Do you remember it – the one in the living room? It has wooden legs and a grey glass top and it's big enough for six people. There are six matching chairs to go with it.

I know you've always liked this furniture so I could let you have it at a good price. I'd rather sell it to you than to a stranger!

Why don't you come around and take another look at them on Saturday? We'll be here all day, so maybe we could have some lunch together?

Give me a ring and let me know,
Love,

Shanda.

TEST B, WRITING TASK 2 (GENERAL TRAINING)

MODEL ANSWER

This model has been prepared by an examiner as an example of a very good answer. However, please note that this is just one example out of many possible approaches.

In many places today, children start primary school at around the age of six or seven. However, because it is more likely now that both parents work, there is little opportunity for children to stay in their own home up to that age. Instead, they will probably go to a nursery school when they are much younger.

While some people think this may be damaging to a child's development, or to a child's relationship with his or her parents, in fact there are many advantages to having school experience at a young age.

Firstly, a child will learn to interact with a lot of different people and some children learn to communicate very early because of this. They are generally more confident and independent than children who stay at home with their parents and who are not used to strangers or new situations. Such children find their first day at school at the age of six very frightening and this may have a negative effect on how they learn.

Another advantage of going to school at an early age is that children develop faster socially. They make friends and learn how to get on with other children of a similar age. This is often not possible at home because they are the only child, or because their brothers or sisters are older or younger.

So overall, I believe that, attending school from a young age is good for most children. They still spend plenty of time at home with their parents, so they can benefit from both environments.

Sample answer sheets

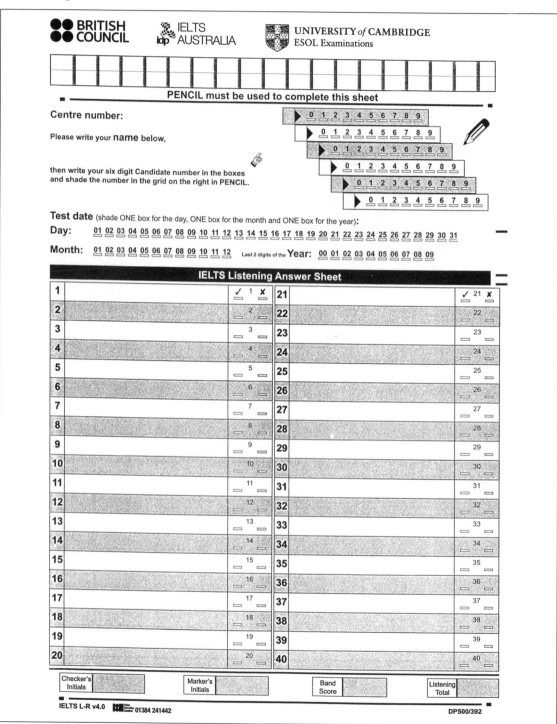

© UCLES 2005 Photocopiable

Are you: Female? ⊂⊃ Male? ⊂⊃

Your first language code: ▶ 0 1 2 3 4 5 6 7 8 9
▶ 0 1 2 3 4 5 6 7 8 9
▶ 0 1 2 3 4 5 6 7 8 9

IELTS Reading Answer Sheet

Module taken (shade one box): Academic ⊂⊃   General Training ⊂⊃

	✓ 1 ✗			✓ 21 ✗
1		**21**		
2	2	**22**		22
3	3	**23**		23
4	4	**24**		24
5	5	**25**		25
6	6	**26**		26
7	7	**27**		27
8	8	**28**		28
9	9	**29**		29
10	10	**30**		30
11	11	**31**		31
12	12	**32**		32
13	13	**33**		33
14	14	**34**		34
15	15	**35**		35
16	16	**36**		36
17	17	**37**		37
18	18	**38**		38
19	19	**39**		39
20	20	**40**		40

Checker's Initials	Marker's Initials	Band Score	Reading Total

Acknowledgements

The author and publishers are grateful to the authors, publishers and others who have given permission for the use of copyright material identified in the text. It has not always been possible to identify the source of material used or to contact the copyright holders and in such cases the publishers would welcome information from the copyright owners.

For the extract on pp. 42–43: from 'Lost for Words' by J Knight, © New Scientist Ltd, 12 August, 2000, and the extract on pp. 50–51: from 'Play's the Thing' by A Baker, © New Scientist Ltd, 9 June, 2001; for the extract on pp. 65–66: from the website www.streetkids.org/micro.htm, 'Micro-Enterprise Credit for Street Youth' by A Sutherland and S Richardson, adapted by kind permission of Street Kids International; for the text on pp. 92–93: adapted from *Archaeology: Theories, Methods and Practice* by Colin Renfrew and Paul Bahn, © 1991 and 1996 Thames and Hudson Ltd, London. Text © 1991 and 1996 Colin Renfrew and Paul Bahn. Adapted by kind permission of Thames and Hudson, London and New York; for the text on pp. 97–98: 'The Problem of Scarce Resources' adapted from *Bioethics in a Liberal Society* by Professor Max Charlesworth, Cambridge University Press, 1993; for the extract on pp. 111–112: 'The History of Early Cinema' from *The Oxford History of World Cinema* edited by Geoffrey Nowell-Smith, © Oxford University Press, 1996.

The publishers are grateful to the following for permission to include photographs:
p. 18: David Wall (davidwallphoto.com); p. 46: Chris Stowers/Panos Pictures; pp. 50 (Helene Rogers) and 71 (John Rettie): Art Directors and TRIP Photo Library; p. 92: Alamy/PHOTOTAKE Inc; p. 126: Spectrum Stock Inc.

Picture research by Valerie Mulcahy
Design concept by Peter Ducker MSTD

Cover design by John Dunne

The cassettes and audio CDs which accompany this book were recorded at Studio AVP, London.